THE TRUTH ABOUT LIBERTY

MANNY EDWARDS, JD

Buffalo Valley, TN

THE TRUTH ABOUT LIBERTY
Copyright © 2011 By Manny Edwards, JD

First Edition

Softcover:
ISBN: 978-0-9836420-0-8
June 2011

eBook:
ISBN: 978-0-9836420-1-5

ePub:
ISBN: 978-0-9836420-2-2

This publication is designed to provide accurate and authoritative information in regard to the subject matter covered. It is sold with the understanding that the publisher is not engaged in rendering legal, accounting, or other professional service. If legal advice or other expert assistance is required, the services of a competent professional person should be sought.

From a Declaration of Principles jointly Adopted by a Committee of the American Bar Association and a Committee of Publishers and Associations

1. Tea Party Movement 2. United States Constitution 3. United States politics and government 4. United States current events 5. United States economic policy 6. United States fiscal aspects 6. United States economic policy 7. United States social policy 8. United States history 9. Title

I. Edwards, JD, Manny II. The Truth About Liberty

The Truth About Liberty may be purchased at special quantity discounts by Tea Party Members or for use as corporate premiums, sales promotions, corporate training programs, gifts, fund raising, book clubs, or educational purposes for schools and universities. For more information contact Mel Cohen, 1000 Pearl Road Pleasantville, TN 37033, 931 593-2484 or email Mel at melcohen@hughes.net.

To reach people around the globe in their own language, we have a rights and licensing department. For translation or reprint rights in English or any other language in book or electronic format contact Mel Cohen, 1000 Pearl Road Pleasantville, TN 37033, 931-593-2484 or email Mel at melcohen@hughes.net.

www.truthaboutliberty.com

TAL Press
Buffalo Valley, TN

Cover design and layout: Lynne Hopwood

THE TRUTH ABOUT LIBERTY

This book is dedicated to my wife,
for whom I strive for liberty.

ACKNOWLEDGMENTS

Mel Cohen and his team for their patience and enthusiasm. All errors are mine.

My agent, Matt Jacobson, for his insightful observations and his friendship.

Dad for his philosophical rigor.

Mom for her support and encouragement.

Jim for his unwavering commitment to liberty.

Tim Wallace for dedicating time and effort to helping me clarify my thinking on difficult issues.

Jake, Nick, Ben, Elizabeth, and Lillianna. I pray they will enjoy whatever blessings of liberty we can secure for them.

Kim; she cheerfully accepted my sudden, drastic, and crazy change of career. Her beauty and sweetness, and her unqualified love and support kept me going.

The great philosophers of liberty who came before, whose work informed mine. I can only mention some of them: Murray N. Rothbard, Hans-Hermann Hoppe, Richard Maybury, Lew Rockwell, Albert J. Nock, John Locke, Thomas Jefferson.

And finally, God himself, for giving us liberty in the first place. May we be grateful, and defend it well.

CONTENTS

1

LIES ABOUT LIBERTY

You've been lied to about your liberty.

You've been told that without the Environmental Protection Agency we would all die from pollution; that without the Department of Education your children wouldn't learn anything; that without Social Security the elderly would starve or freeze; that without invasive body searches by the Transportation Security Administration airplanes would fall out of the sky; that without the Food and Drug Administration your food would be poisoned; that without the state and federal courts you would have no justice; and that without Obamacare you wouldn't get medical treatment.

You've been told that the only alternative to chaos is a government that regulates everything. The founders of the United States of America risked all they had to "secure the blessings of liberty," but you've been told that liberty is an obstacle to food, warmth, knowledge, air, medical care, justice, and security. You've been told that your blessings come from the government.

The truth is that *free people* provide all these things far more abundantly than totalitarian government. To satisfy their lust for power and money, Republicans and Democrats together have built up the colossal government we have now—an all-encompassing regulatory network that affects every aspect of your life, every day, every time you turn around. Every breath you take, there's the government. The kind of welfare-warfare-socialist-police state we associate with Nazi Germany and the old Soviet Union has now conquered the land of the free.

Consider:

– The Transportation Security Administration hires pedophiles and other sex offenders who routinely engage in government-sanctioned sexual assault of adults and children.[1]

– Police officers in SWAT uniforms storm barber shops with guns drawn (*without* a warrant), handcuff people and make them lie on the floor, ransack the place and destroy property under the guise of looking for a license to practice barbering.[2]

– Police officers raid organic grocery stores with guns drawn and pointed at customers. What was the dangerous contraband they sought? Raw milk. In the USA, food is a controlled substance.[3]

– The IRS takes your money and gives it to Planned Parenthood, which performed over 332,000 abortions in 2009. It doesn't matter if you think abortion is murder – you have to pay for it anyway.[4]

---

1 Paul Joseph Watson, "TSA Gives Rapists And Illegals The Green Light While Groping Children," *Alex Jones' Prison Planet*, Nov. 10, 2010 (http://www.prisonplanet.com/tsa-gives-rapists-and-illegals-the-green-light-while-groping-children.html).

2 Tonyaa Weathersbee, "Barber Shop Raids Recall Days of Slavery," *Black America Web*, Dec. 15, 2010 (http://www.blackamericaweb.com/?q=articles%2Fnews%2Fbaw_commentary_news%2F24305&sms_ss=facebook&at_x).

3 P.J. Huffstutter, "Raw Milk Raid Highlights A Hunger," *Los Angeles Times*, July 25, 2010 (http://articles.latimes.com/2010/jul/25/business/la-fi-raw-food-raid-20100725). Watch a video of the raid at *Republic Broadcasting Network* (http://republicbroadcasting. org/?p=9870). On the health benefits of raw milk, see Randolph Jonsson, "Finally! Raw Milk Information You Can Trust!" *Raw Milk Facts* (http://www.raw-milk-facts.com/index.html). On the negative health consequences of pasteurization laws, see Kerri Knox, "The Long Term Health Consequences of Pasteurized Milk Laws, *Easy Immune System Health Blog*, (http://blog.easy-immune-health.com/digestive-health/the-long-term-health-consequences-of-pasteurized-milk-laws). The Weston A. Price Foundation is one of the most important sources of information about natural foods and nutrition; http://www.westonaprice.org.

4 As of this writing, 2009 is the latest year for which Planned Parenthood has published figures. Penny Starr, "Planned Parenthood Reports Abortion Rate Up By More Than 8,000 in One Year," *CNS News*, March 7, 2011 (http://www.cnsnews.com/news/article/planned-parenthood-reports-record-aborti).

– According to Boston University economist Laurence Kotlikoff, social security has an unfunded obligation (above the amount which we're already being taxed) of over $200 trillion.[5] This is four times the total private wealth of the United States. It's the biggest Ponzi scheme in history. Social security is doomed, yet we're still paying for it.

– On the idea that people are state property, they are subjected to forced medical care,[6] and now under Obamacare you'll be forced to buy the health insurance the government tells you to buy. For your own good, of course.

---

5 Laurence Kotlikoff, "U.S. Is Bankrupt and We Don't Even Know It: Laurence Kotlikoff," Bloomberg News, Aug. 10, 2010 (http://www.bloomberg.com/news/2010-08-11/u-s-is-bankrupt-and-we-don-t-even-know-commentary-by-laurence-kotlikoff.html). I don't know the math to verify this stunning claim, but because of his credentials I don't reject it out of hand. Laurence J. Kotlikoff is a William Fairfield Warren Professor at Boston University, a Professor of Economics at Boston University, a Fellow of the American Academy of Arts and Sciences, a Fellow of the Econometric Society, a Research Associate of the National Bureau of Economic Research, President of Economic Security Planning, Inc., a company specializing in financial planning software, a columnist for Bloomberg, a columnist for Forbes, and a blogger for The Economist. Professor Kotlikoff received his B.A. in Economics from the University of Pennsylvania in 1973 and his Ph.D. in Economics from Harvard University in 1977.

From 1977 through 1983 he served on the faculties of economics of the University of California, Los Angeles and Yale University. In 1981-82 Professor Kotlikoff was a Senior Economist with the President's Council of Economic Advisers.

Professor Kotlikoff is author or co-author of 14 books and hundreds of professional journal articles.

Professor Kotlikoff publishes extensively in newspapers and magazines on issues of financial reform, personal finance, taxes, Social Security, healthcare, deficits, generational accounting, pensions, saving, and insurance.

Professor Kotlikoff has served as a consultant to the International Monetary Fund, the World Bank, the Harvard Institute for International Development, the Organization for Economic Cooperation and Development, the Swedish Ministry of Finance, the Norwegian Ministry of Finance, the Bank of Italy, the Bank of Japan, the Bank of England, the Government of Russia, the Government of Ukraine, the Government of Bolivia, the Government of Bulgaria, the Treasury of New Zealand, the Office of Management and Budget, the U.S. Department of Education, the U.S. Department of Labor, the Joint Committee on Taxation, The Commonwealth of Massachusetts, The American Council of Life Insurance, Merrill Lynch, Fidelity Investments, AT&T, AON Corp., and other major U.S. corporations.

He has provided expert testimony on numerous occasions to committees of Congress including the Senate Finance Committee, the House Ways and Means Committee, and the Joint Economic Committee.

Andrew Jackson warned that "eternal vigilance is the price of liberty." Imagine holding something so dear that you're willing to pledge "eternal vigilance" to preserve it. Our forefathers pledged their lives, their fortunes, and their sacred honor to secure the blessings of liberty for themselves and their posterity. But those men were very different from the politicians you find today.

The Republican leadership doesn't have Andrew Jackson's dedication to liberty. Afraid of the media, afraid of losing their place in the ruling class, afraid to stand firm for anything, they have lost their foundation in principles of limited government. They have no zeal, no passion, no courage, and no vision, and so there's no one in Washington to resist the state's relentless assault on our liberty.

We're so far from the scope of liberties our founders had that you have to re-calibrate your mind even to grasp the differences. A tweak here and there won't restore our liberties.

We have to hit the reset button.

Restoring liberty is going to require a complete paradigm shift. If we have learned anything from the constantly compromising Republicans, it is that if we're going to regain our liberties, we will have to dedicate ourselves to radical changes, not incremental ones. Then we might merely obtain incremental changes in the direction of greater liberty. If we only try to get small tax reductions, we might only end up with small tax increases.

For generations we have called for "common sense" in government spending, but the waste, stupidity, and corruption have only worsened. The welfare explosion has

---

6 William Norman Grigg, "Stormtroopers and Child-Snatchers," *LewRockwell.com*, April 13, 2011 (http://www.lewrockwell.com/grigg/grigg-w206.html).

engulfed the whole nation and bankrupted us. The national debt is so enormous that it cannot be comprehended. The dollar is the weakest in history, as the world, knowing full well that our economy is on the brink, sells it off in panic to buy gold, silver and foreign currencies. We can't reason with the politicians anymore. We can't debate and negotiate for more sensible spending. It's too late for that; the only thing we can do now is stop them, cut them off, turn off the tap. They have to stop spending.

It is not enough to merely reduce the income tax; we must be committed to eliminating it entirely. The income tax was a wretched idea from the beginning; it makes us slaves of the government for several months every year.

We must be committed not just to reducing deficit spending, we much stop it immediately. Our Tea Party candidates won the 2010 election on a promise to cut spending by a measly $100 billion, but the Republican leadership wouldn't even do that much for us, and delivered only $38 billion in cuts instead. When they announced this with great pomp, they said this was the best deal that could be gotten after a hard fight.

The sad thing is, they weren't kidding. The Republican leadership lives in a different universe than we do, one in which this failure is called a great accomplishment. When our government is spending that much every four days and running a $38 billion *deficit* every nine days, calling this a victory is frankly pathetic. As Sarah Palin once suggested, if they won't fight like men, they should at least learn to fight like girls.

We must be committed to eliminating the income tax *and also* the deficit – we're looking for a radical, game-changing reduction in the size of the federal government, not little incremental ones. One thing we'd better learn from the radical left is that to accomplish radical change you have to take a radical position.

We're not looking for little improvements, but drastic ones. We want to *eliminate* the IRS, the EPA, and the Department of Education. We want to End the Fed and return to commodity money, even competitive money systems. Eliminate the TSA completely and let the airlines and their insurance companies provide security in a competitive market – it will be more effective, less intrusive, *and* less expensive.

Obviously, change of this magnitude might not occur immediately, but we must continually maintain that it *should*, and all the while fight for it, accepting the smaller victories if they're all we can get, but never remaining satisfied with them.

We certainly won't find this mindset in the Republican Party leadership. Only the grassroots, the Tea Party, has the ability *right now* to bring about this kind of radical change. Tea partiers are energized, dissatisfied with the status quo, and frustrated with the Republicans, who are spineless, feckless, and inconsistent in the fight for liberty, and often even hostile to it.

But we must understand that we don't have unlimited resources. We won't be able to marshall this kind of energy indefinitely – we need to choose our battles carefully.

For now, we in the Tea Party are fighting for a return to a more conservative position, such as what we had in the 80s or maybe the 50s. But resetting things back to 1980 only wins us thirty years, and then we'll have to fight for another reset all over again. Many of us will have to fight this battle twice. I don't know about you, but I don't like to fight over the same ground more than once.

Our objective must be not just a little less oppression, but liberty on a grand scale. We have the will, the energy, and the means, but there is one thing we still lack – a coherent set of core principles that, if put into practice, will actually achieve lasting liberty. But to understand what these principles must be, we must first understand what we're fighting against; we must understand just how free we are *not*, so let's look at a day in the life of Joe Freeman.

———∞∞∞———

Joe wakes up before dawn and turns on a light. It's an incandescent bulb, one of the last he'll be able to buy because, starting in 2012, it will be illegal to sell them. After that date, he'll have to buy more expensive fluorescent bulbs that contain toxic substances.

Now, maybe you say that's good because it'll force Joe to use less electricity. Maybe you think that consuming a lot of electricity is bad for the environment, and the environment is more important than Joe's liberty. If so, let me point out two things; first, Joe and a lot of other people don't think using energy has a bad impact on the environment, and second, the producer of the light bulb is the one who owns it, and for the government to tell him he can't sell it is tyrannical.

In any event, all we're doing for now is recognizing the fact that Joe will soon lose the freedom to choose an incandescent bulb.

For breakfast Joe has milk, eggs, and bacon. The milk is pasteurized because it is illegal for dairies to sell unpasteurized milk. Knowing that they will have to pasteurize it anyway, the dairies don't handle the milk with the same care as a small farmer who intends to drink it raw, so Joe consumes a lot of sterilized garbage in his milk. He would like to drink raw milk because he believes there are many health benefits, but he lives in a town with zoning laws that forbid him to keep a cow. He could legally buy a "herd-share" of a small farmer's herd, and then he would technically own the milk. Then he could pay a "handling fee" to the farmer and obtain raw milk that way, but it comes to $8 a gallon, a price he cannot afford.

Some people might say that's better for him anyway, but Joe doesn't want you or anyone else to tell him what he must or must not eat "for his own good." In a free country, you can choose pasteurized milk for yourself because you think it's better, and Joe can choose raw milk because he thinks that's better. That's liberty. As it is, others have deprived Joe of his liberty because they've taken it upon themselves to decide what's best for him.

Joe's wife, Sarah, sets the breakfast table, but first she has to re-wash the dishes. As she takes them out of the dishwasher, there are still particles of food on them. It's a new dishwasher, and it works exactly as designed, but to comply with federal regulations it was designed to use a miniscule amount of unheated water; even after a nearly three-hour wash cycle the night before, the dishes aren't clean. And because it has no heater element, they're still wet in the morning, so she has to dry them by hand.

Joe's eggs are pale and rather tasteless, unlike the eggs with rich, firm, orange yolks he gathered from his own chickens when he was a child. Independently raised "farm eggs" are expensive compared to store-bought eggs; small farmers have a hard time competing with the industrial egg farms not because their eggs are not as good – they're actually better – but because the government has given the big egg farms special privileges. They get subsidies. Joe's tax dollars go to "Big Egg," which makes their eggs cheaper. Because competitors don't get subsidies, it makes their eggs more expensive, so Big Egg doesn't have to work harder to make good eggs; with the subsidy, Joe has already paid for a fraction of the eggs in the supermarket, so he figures he might as well finish buying them.

Same for Joe's bacon. "Big Pork" is so heavily regulated by the government that profit would be impossible if it had to actually compete in a free market. Fortunately for those few big industrial pork processing operations, they don't have anything to worry about; in addition to government subsidies, they got the government to pass laws forbidding farmers from raising pigs for sale to the public. It's actually illegal for someone to start a new hog-raising operation in Joe's state.

While Joe is pondering this, his wife tells him the toilet is clogged again. For several years it has been illegal for toilet manufacturers to make toilets that flush more than 1.6 gallons of water at a time. Joe's house was built in the 1960s and has 4-inch main drain pipes, which are fine if you flush more water through them, but when they bought the house, Joe's wife redecorated and had to buy the new toilets with inadequate water flushing capacity. They didn't realize what a headache that was going to be. They have to flush twice whenever they use the toilet, but sometimes the kids forget.

After plunging the toilet, Joe goes to work. He owns a graphics business with ten employees. His first meeting is with two employees he's going to lay off. Obamacare regulations have caused his health insurance carrier to increase their premiums, and this increased cost is about to raise the rate of unemployment in his town.

Some of Joe's tax dollars will support the laid off employees for several months while they look for a job that pays more than their unemployment checks. One of them will decide it's not worth the trouble, because on welfare they'll give him almost as much as he would earn by working. He'd rather make up the difference with a little easy, undeclared, cash-only yard work. Before he started collecting checks from the government, he would never have considered cheating on his taxes, but now he figures, since they're already giving him money, it's no big deal to just hang on to a few more bucks. Thus, welfare corrupts the recipient.

At about 10 o'clock that morning, Joe's stomach is feeling a little upset, and his wife has told him it's probably from drinking homogenized milk. There's no law against selling unhomogenized milk, but it's almost impossible to find pasteurized milk from the industrial dairies that hasn't also been homogenized. Joe has heard about a small farmer ten miles away who sells raw milk for only $6 a gallon, instead of $8, so he places a call. The farmer is dealing with a visit from the FDA; he doesn't answer the phone, so Joe leaves a message.

Joe goes to lunch with a client who says he's not going to buy any more of the product safety labels Joe has been printing for him, because the Product Safety Commission (PSC) is putting the client out of business. The client manufactures plastic household buckets for mopping and such. Someone bought the bucket and turned it upside down to use it as a stepping stool to reach a coffee cup in a high cupboard. The bucket collapsed, the cup broke on the kitchen floor, and the person lost her sight in the right eye when a shard flew into it. She filed a lawsuit, and a local jury with good common sense threw the case out, but the federal PSC bureaucrat in Washington, DC, fined Joe's client anyway for failing to include a label telling people not to use the bucket as a stepping stool. The fine bankrupted Joe's client, so he can't buy Joe's labels anymore. Joe considers laying off another employee.

On his way back to the office, Joe stops to buy gas and pays more than twice as much as he should have to. The government taxes every gallon as it comes out of the pump. It also taxes every gallon as it comes out of the well. The Big Oil company pays 35% in corporate taxes, and then the shareholders pay taxes on the dividends. The refinery has other government-added expenses because it has to manufacture not just the types of fuel people want to buy; it has to make about 90 different formulations for different areas of the country to comply with conflicting government air pollution standards. All these added costs increase the price of gas.[7]

Joe decides to go inside the store to buy some bubble gum for his son. He has a permit to carry a handgun, but he leaves the gun in the car, because it's illegal to carry a gun into a store that sells alcohol, and this store sells beer. While he's inside, someone else comes in with a gun and commits a robbery. He takes the money in the cash register and every customer's money, including Joe's. The criminal knew it was illegal to take guns into stores that sell alcohol, and this made the "gun-free zone" a good target. He figured rightly that no one in the store could stop him from committing a robbery, because they wouldn't be armed.

The criminal gets away and Joe leaves without the bubble gum.

The gas station's insurance company increases its premium. This adds a little more to the cost of gas. In addition,

---

7 This doesn't even address the hidden costs of engine damage caused by government-mandated ethanol/gasoline formulations.

customers in the area avoid that station because it now has a reputation for being in a "bad neighborhood." That particular gas station now sells less gas and eventually closes. With less competition now, the gas station a block away increases its price a few cents, and everyone has to pay more for gas. The poor get jealous of richer people and a politician comes along promising to tax them more. He gets elected and levies a new city tax on gas stations. To cover the added cost, the gas stations charge a little more for gas, and everyone loses a little more money. However, this hurts the poor more than the rich; the increased cost of gasoline is a larger marginal expense for the poor man than it is for the rich man. So the poor, because they resented the rich, make the rich a little poorer, but they make themselves poorer too. They don't really think about this very hard, though – they're just happy their politician stuck it to the rich.

All this because it was illegal for citizens to take a gun into a gas station that sells beer.

Later, the criminal will be caught robbing a bank. Joe, the small dairy farmer, the bankrupt bucket manufacturer, and the laid-off employees will pay for the criminal's trial. This includes the judge's salary and that of the entire courthouse staff, the prosecution and its support staff, and even the attorney appointed to defend the criminal. Then they will pay to house, feed, and clothe the criminal. After a short time the criminal will be released and he will briefly enter a tax-paid job search program. The only people who might hire him aren't willing to pay him very much, but it's illegal to pay him less than the government-mandated "minimum wage," so no one offers him a job and he resumes committing robberies.

This criminal will die by gunshot while breaking into someone's house late one night. The homeowner, who was shot by the criminal but survived, will spend eight years in prison, because in his city it is illegal to possess a shotgun. His neighbors, who paid for his trial, will also pay to house, clothe, and feed him. His children will go on welfare and the neighbors will pay for that too. Three years after he goes to prison, his wife will divorce him.

Meanwhile, gun control advocates will call for even more laws making it illegal to possess even more kinds of guns. Some citizens will mention the Second Amendment, which forbids the government to infringe the right to keep and bear arms, but they don't work very hard to express their concerns. The highly organized, activist gun control advocates paint them as kooks, and the concerned citizens are uncomfortable being regarded as "gun nuts." They trade their liberty for maintaining a good public image.

The gun control advocates win the day. They get more laws passed; fewer good citizens have guns, but the criminals still have them because they never cared about gun control laws in the first place. Fearing for his safety, the rich director of the gun control group hires armed bodyguards to protect him.

Joe is shaken up after the gas station robbery and doesn't feel like going back to the office, so he drives home instead. He calls ahead to tell his wife what happened, and he spends quite a few minutes calming her down and then asking her to call and cancel his stolen debit card. While he's still talking, Joe gets pulled over by a cop who is enforcing a new law making it illegal to talk on a cell phone while driving. The cop approaches Joe and sees the gun in the passenger seat. Instead of assuming that Joe is a good citizen, he's rude and acts like a bully because he's "tough on crime" and is suspicious of anyone who has a gun but not a badge.

Joe can't produce his permit for the gun because it was stolen at the gas station when the crook took his wallet. The cop knows about the robbery, but he confiscates the gun anyway under a "zero tolerance" policy. He tells Joe he'll have to file a claim at the police station once he proves he has a permit on file. Joe doesn't know it yet, but there was a recent computer system upgrade at the state capital, and many driver's license and gun permit records were lost. The upgrade was unnecessary, but the computer company was run by the brother of one of the state legislators, and Joe's taxes helped pay for the sloppy computer upgrade contract in which the records were lost. By the time he proves he was legally in possession, his gun has been "lost," and although he files a claim, it gets buried in a bureaucratic black hole designed to hide the corruption surrounding the disappearance of millions of dollars worth of confiscated property.

Before he leaves, the cop gives Joe a citation for having an illegal cell phone conversation.

Finally back home, Joe sinks into his chair, feeling very old. His wife brings him a nice herbal tea, and he begins to relax. The phone rings.

It's the farmer returning Joe's call. Joe asks if he can buy some raw milk. Unfortunately, the farmer happens to live across the state line, and he tells Joe he just found out it's illegal to deliver raw milk from one state to another for human consumption. Joe says he won't tell anyone, but that's irrelevant, the farmer says, because the FDA has fined him a year's worth of income, confiscated his equipment and livestock, and filed an injunction to shut down his business.

2

THE KINGS OF AMERICA

A totalitarian government has the power to control anything and everything. In the United States, the government has the power to forbid you to grow a crop. If you do it anyway they can destroy your crop and fine you. And I'm not talking about marijuana. I'm talking about food.

If you read the Constitution, you won't find this power granted to the government. In fact, its power is extremely limited; it has only 18 enumerated powers.[8] So if the government has only 18 powers, and none of these is the power to tell you what food you can or cannot raise for yourself, how does the government get away with doing so anyway?

They simply ignore the Constitution. Rulers like power. The Constitution limits their power, so they ignore it.

The Judicial branch of the government is complicit in all this. In the case of Wickard v. Filburn,[9] the Supreme Court interpreted the Constitution so as to completely negate its limitations of power. This case established the government's virtually unfettered power to control anything and everything under the Constitution's commerce clause.

---

8 U.S. Constitution, Article 1, Section 8.

9 317 U.S. 111 (1942).

One of the 18 enumerated powers is the power to regulate interstate commerce. To define "interstate commerce" the Supreme Court adopted the "economic effect" test, which says basically "if your activity affects interstate commerce, then Congress has the power to regulate it." So if you blow your nose in your sleeve instead of buying a box of tissues, you are depriving the tissue-maker of a sale, and Congress can make it illegal to blow your nose in your sleeve.

Everything you do affects interstate commerce, so Congress can regulate everything, and the limitation of powers in the Constitution means nothing. Whether the government actually does regulate some particular activity or not depends only on the political whims of the moment. Today people might not support a ban on blowing your nose in your sleeve, but tomorrow they might.[10] Our only security against totalitarian government was the list of power limitations in the Constitution, and now they're gone.

People in the government live by different rules than the ones we have to live by, so they are not "representative" of the people. On the contrary, they have special privileges, and they dispense special privileges to some groups of people in exchange for political power.

The people who founded this nation did not trust a powerful government. We get disgusted when giant corporations get special favors from the government, like ethanol subsidies, for example, because we pay via taxes for the government to simply give a rich corporation giant sums

---

10 This is not hyperbole. Imagine that we're victims of a pandemic flu, and the government issues emergency regulations "in the public interest." Among these might be mandatory flu shots, face masks, and certain mandatory hygienic practices such as hand-washing and the use of facial tissues, perhaps only FDA approved tissues manufactured by a small cartel of Big Pharma companies. Not so hard to imagine, is it?

of money. We might then argue about whether the CEOs are to blame for corrupting the government or vice versa, but the point is that the problem is power. The problem vanishes if we just deny the government the power to dispense the favors. If the government can't dispense subsidies, we don't have to worry about whether it's the politician or the CEO who's corrupt – it becomes irrelevant.

People in government have a privilege no other human institution has; they can use *force* to take money from others. This privilege is the basis of what we call "political power," and the founders knew from personal experience that it's a very dangerous power to give anyone, because taxation is theft with an illusion of legitimacy. This illusion is maintained by persuading enough citizens that the theft is necessary in order to avoid some worse calamity. For example, they say that if there were no taxes there would be no roads, no security from terrorists, no education, and that children and the elderly would starve. When people hear this they get scared, and although they would normally not want to steal, they figure it must be done to avoid these fearsome events.

The founders understood that government should never be trusted. They wanted a government in which they might have *confidence*, because its power was so limited that it would never be a threat to our liberties, but they never expected anyone to *trust* it.

For this reason, they created a Constitution with two fundamental characteristics to keep the government under control. First, they severely limited the kinds of power the government could exercise. This is the reason for the section that enumerates the powers of the government. The idea was that the government would only do those things which are enumerated in that section, but those limitations are now universally ignored by all branches of government.

Second, the founders designed the government purposely to be ineffective, to make it very difficult for it to pass legislation, or in fact to accomplish much of anything. Our government is deliberately not good at governing, because the founders didn't want it to rule us, they just wanted the government to be there so some other government wouldn't come along and start ruling over us. The government designed by our founders was not much more than a placeholder, filling a sort of vacuum in which people think a government must exist.

The government was never meant to be very effective or have much power, which is why they designed it following the principle of separation of powers. The government is composed of three branches; the executive branch, the legislative branch, and the judicial branch. Constitutionally, none of these branches of government can accomplish much without the cooperation of the other branches, and none of them can do the things the other branches are supposed to do.

This is a terribly inefficient way to govern. If you want streamlined government, you remove all the obstacles in the way of getting things done; you certainly don't deliberately impede the legislative and executive processes. In fact, to really get things done efficiently, you give one man (or him and his lieutenants) all the power to make laws and enforce them.

However, this is not at all how our government was structured. For example, under the Constitution, only the legislative branch can create the laws that govern our behavior. This limitation is a serious obstacle to power-hungry rulers, and so it is completely ignored. The executive branch operates "executive agencies" like the FDA, FCC, and the FAA. These agencies pass laws, even though only the legislature is supposed to do that. They call the laws "rules," but they are indistinguishable from laws.

Congress gets around constitutional restrictions by claiming "oversight" authority over these agencies, but that's really just a sham. If elected officials passed these unpopular laws they would lose the next election, so they delegate the task to the executive agencies. The people who make the laws in those agencies are unelected bureaucrats. If they happen to create a rule that is very unpopular, Congress calls for "hearings" where they can pontificate and criticize and point fingers and look good for their voters. The bureaucrat takes his lumps – he understands this game – and then everyone goes home. Nothing changes.

Now we even have "czars," like the drug czar, appointed by the president without approval of the legislative branch. No one knows how much they get paid unless the president chooses to tell us, and no one knows precisely what they do or what powers they've been given, unless the president chooses to tell us. It's no coincidence that they chose the title "czar;" it means "caesar." If they had any concern for liberty, they would be ashamed to bear the title or the responsibilities of their office.

Another example; the executive branch is supposed to spend only the money the legislative branch specifically approves. But in fact, the legislature routinely grants the executive branch big blocks of money to spend completely at its discretion. The $700 billion Troubled Asset Relief Program is a recent example which led to the nationalization of General Motors.

The function of the judicial branch is to interpret the Constitution and laws of the United States, but it has abdicated this responsibility. Instead of determining the meaning of what the Constitution says, the federal courts routinely reinvent it, justifying their action by saying that if the founders had known what the future would bring they would have written the Constitution to account for it.

The thing is, the founders did predict the future, and provided a constitutional process of amendment to allow the people to change the Constitution if needed. They deliberately made this very difficult to do, but people in the government don't like this limitation on their power. They want more power than the Constitution allows, and so they simply ignore the amendment process and seize the power they want.

As mentioned, the judiciary is complicit in the consolidation of government power, but this is no surprise since the government has a monopoly on the administration of justice (you can't go to just anybody and have him declare a federal law unconstitutional; it has to be a federal judge). In determining the scope and reach of federal power, you can only appeal to the federal government. The federal judiciary is a federal institution with a monopoly on the administration of justice, so when you go to the federal court to find out how much power the federal government has, you're going to get a result that favors the federal government. Sure, there will be occasional exceptions, but just look at the expansion of federal power since this nation was founded.

Politicians justify their power grabs by saying that what they're doing is very important, and so they need the government to run efficiently. This argument is often framed around the issue of security in one way or another; food must be inspected by the government to keep us safe; water must be regulated by the government to keep us safe; gasoline must be regulated by the government to keep the air clean; airline security must be managed by the government to keep boogiemen from crashing airplanes on our heads. Unfortunately (say the Statists[11]), the Constitution has created all sorts of inefficiencies in the government which make it ineffective. It's an obstacle to our security.

Citizens then become afraid of inefficiency and forget that government inefficiency is one of the safeguards of their liberty. So they ignore the Constitution and trade liberty for the illusion of government-provided security. If we were in charge of our own security we could guard against all assaults on our liberties, no matter where they came from, but now that the government is in charge of security, who will provide security from the government?

With the government in charge of security and no constitutional limitations, there's no limit now to what it can do. If a majority of the people want an unconstitutional social security program, they go to the government and get it.

If a majority wants an unconstitutional education system, they get it.

If a majority wants unconstitutional gun control, they get it.

If a majority wants unconstitutional laws about what food you eat, what cars you drive, what kind of toilets and dishwashers you install in your house, and countless other infringements on your liberties, they get it.

Now that they have these powers, they've gone even farther – now they even rule *against* the will of the majority. Obamacare was passed against the will of a large majority, but it made no difference. The Federal Reserve was created without the knowledge of most of the people, and certainly

---

11 A statist is one who believes that the state, instead of the private sector, is the solution to economic, social, and cultural problems.

without their understanding of the catastrophic consequences to our economy and our liberty.

As of this writing, President Obama has directed the EPA to enact carbon emission regulations that were rejected by Congress. What he couldn't do by the constitutional law-making process, he is doing by decree. He's just dictating the result he wants. He's a dictator.

It should now be clear that we don't really have representatives in the government. A representative stands in the place of another in relation to a third party. For instance, suppose my neighbor invites me to his house to discuss building a fence on our mutual property line, but I can't attend; I might send someone, perhaps my son, to speak for me. I tell him he can agree to share the cost of a fence up to a total of $1000. He's my representative to the neighbor, and his authority is limited by my instructions.

But when we elect a candidate to office, he doesn't *represent* us to the government; he becomes a *member of* the government. He becomes our ruler, and we the ruled. He passes laws that apply to us but not to him. He collects taxes from us and pays himself a handsome salary. He travels in great style. He uses our money to create favors for people who promise votes in return, so he can stay in office and keep collecting more money and more power.

This is not representation. It is tyranny.

I am not advocating a violent revolution; I hope to prevent one. But you have to understand that revolution – whether peaceful or violent – is inevitable in this country. Americans are descended from people who risked their lives to come to the New World and then took up arms against rulers just like the ones we have today. While we have lost many liberties, and while a large segment of our population is not concerned about it, many are waking up to the assaults against liberty they live with every day. In many families the older generations have passed down stories about their ancestors, stories of the glory and blessings of liberty. When they hear what they have lost they burn with anger and indignation, and this anger is, not surprisingly, directed at those who took their liberties.

The only way to regain our liberties without taking up arms is to act soon, while there is still the possibility of a peaceful revolution. If we don't, it will soon be impossible, because the government is dismantling the constitutional limitations of power which were the only thing that prevented tyranny.

There is still time to fix this peacefully. But you can't wait any longer.

3

LIBERTY AND THE STATE

To compel a man to furnish contributions of money for the propagation of opinions which he disbelieves and abhors, is sinful and tyrannical.

— Thomas Jefferson

If you don't know what the founders of our nation believed about liberty, you can understand neither the kind of government they established, nor why they broke away from England in the first place. According to them, liberty is a gift from the creator. Governments do not create liberty; they can only protect it or infringe upon it.

The founders held that liberty could not be contained in legislation. It is a relational condition. The proper function of government was to safeguard that relationship between the citizens of a nation.

Today this seems to be a radical view of government, but it's precisely what the founders of the United States believed. This is easy to prove just by studying the Constitution, the Federalist Papers, the Anti-Federalist Papers, and the Declaration of Independence. The anti-federalists believed that there should be no federal government at all, because it would grow out of control and rule tyrannically over the people. The federalists feared that if they didn't create a government, someone else would, and tyrannical government would rise anyway. They proposed to create a weak federal government, and persuaded the anti-federalists to go along.

It turns out the anti-federalists were right; the government has broken free of the limitations of the Constitution and now rules over us far beyond its founding mandate.

How did this happen? What is the underlying cause of our loss of liberties? How did we go from being a country that championed liberty above all else, to one that is much like the socialist governments of Europe and the tin-pot dictatorships of Africa and South America, and in some ways much worse?

Statism is the idea that the state is the solution to life's problems. If there are poor people in the neighborhood, the free man sees charity, education, and a work ethic as the solution; the statist takes money from people by force (taxation) and gives it to the poor man (welfare). If the young have difficult working conditions, the free man offers them a better job; the statist bans all child labor by law, depriving children of economic opportunity. If a free man is concerned about the welfare of sea cucumbers, he finds like-minded people and persuades them to pool their resources to protect them; the statist confiscates money from people who have other concerns. The statist solution always deprives people of their money and their liberty.

States are by far the greatest obstacle to liberty in our experience. Consider your own circumstances. Just tally up the limitations on your liberty in your everyday activities;

what you're forbidden or required to do, the fees and taxes you pay, the construction codes and environmental regulations you have to comply with, your limited choices in buying fuel, electricity, and other public utilities. If you run a business, consider the volumes of regulations that limit your opportunities, such as how you relate to employees, suppliers, and customers. You'll find there is almost nothing about your business that is not restricted in some way by the state. Whatever you think of the need for airline security, it is indisputably intrusive. Regardless of how workable private road systems might be, it is indisputable that you have essentially no opportunity to experiment with them. In all these cases the source of the restrictions on your liberties is not a force outside our borders, but our very own government.

Statism thrives on greed and laziness. People become jealous of the wealth of others and demand that the government take money from the rich and give it to them. We get higher taxes, welfare, food stamps, and social security, and, because states can't tax enough to pay for all this, we also get big deficits. At the other end of the spectrum, rich corporations are seduced by government officials who promise big profits in exchange for political power. These corporations are enticed or even coerced into supporting legislation that give the politicians control over us, and we get the robber barons, big monopolies, big subsidies – what we call "crony capitalism." Or maybe the corporations pressure the government for grants, favors, and subsidies, because it's easier than competing in a free market. But whether the corruption begins with the politician or the corporate CEO, either way the fundamental problem is that the state has the power to dispense these privileges in the first place.

The state never becomes less intrusive; we always see *increasing* restrictions on our liberty because neither of the main political parties is ever interested in reducing its power. The Democrats (liberal/left) want big government so they can restrict markets and redistribute wealth. The Republicans (conservative/right) want big government so they can control morals and subsidize giant corporations. Both parties conduct foreign wars to funnel money to defense contractors, and also for the thrill of it. Thus, as the government changes hands from one election cycle to the next, all we get is more big government. Sometimes it grows more quickly or a bit more slowly, but it never shrinks.

After several generations of this constant expansion, the state has its hand in every aspect of our lives; it controls how fast you drive, how efficient your car must be, the amount of oil you can drill for and where you can drill for it.

It controls insurance companies, food processing, agriculture, construction, insurance of every kind, manufacturing of every kind, banking, the money supply, education, healthcare, unions, communications, the airwaves, the airlines, and forestry.

It has regulations about product labeling, working conditions, compensation for the work done, telephones, televisions, radios, home appliances, pets, lawn mowers, and outdoor grills.

It controls what your children learn and what kind of medical care you get.

A generation ago, if you wanted to build a bridge across your ditch you just built it, but today you have to get permission from the state. You can't even get married without state permission.

And yet, what have we gained in exchange for our liberty? The state has not improved education; it has not abolished poverty; it has not abolished inflation; it has not improved race relations; it has not ended wars; it has not stopped the drug trade; it has not improved security; it has not reduced the cost of healthcare.

The state never improves these things; it is not capable of doing so. All it does is fool people into thinking it can provide solutions, but the only thing it actually does is deprive us of liberty and take control of our lives.

The state is the natural enemy of liberty. Political power attracts more power. Indeed, people in power will seize more power by any means they can get away with, whether it's legal or not, no matter what a Constitution says.

We've been trained to take for granted that the state is the solution to our problems, but we need to learn to think like a free people. Let's check in on Joe Freeman again.

There was a dry summer in Joe's state. When he took his family camping in his RV one weekend, he loaded his camping gear, including a big bag of charcoal and some hot dogs. When they arrived at the RV park, he was told there was a ban on open-air fires; he'll have to cook his hot dogs in the RV. Joe said he can boil his hot dogs any time, but he wants them roasted over a fire, so he told the park manager he was canceling his reservation to go to a park that allowed open air fires. That's when the manager told him that he'd have to drive out of state, because it was a state-wide ban imposed by the state itself.

Never mind that Joe is responsible and knows how to keep his fire in the fire ring. Never mind that wild fires don't usually start in RV parks that are supervised by the attendants and populated with other concerned campers; they start in the woods or fields when irresponsible campers don't carefully tend the fire. Never mind that these irresponsible people are by definition irresponsible in the first place and won't heed the ban, and there will be camp fires getting out of control anyway.

The problem is that there is a handful of irresponsible people out there, and the statist solution is to ban everyone from lighting an open air fire. So thousands of campers will be forbidden to light camp fires, and this restriction on everyone's liberty won't even accomplish its stated purpose; it won't prevent wildfires.

There is another way. It is possible to discourage irresponsibility in tending campfires without restricting everyone's liberty for the sake of a half-dozen careless people.

Let's see how this might work in a free society.

It has been a dry summer in Joe's state. Mosquitoes are almost nonexistent, the days are deep blue and sunny, the nights are clear and cool, and it seems like a great weekend for camping. So Joe, Sarah, and the kids load the RV and head to their favorite RV park. They are looking forward to roasting hot dogs and playing games around the campfire.

When they check in, the manager tells Joe that the drought has created a fire hazard. The park ranger had called him and asked him to caution his guests, since many of them will be traveling from other states and might not know of the increased risks. The manager earns his living running this park and has every incentive to ensure the safety of the people and their property, not to mention his own. He doesn't need a law telling him this; his pecuniary interest in the park and his own moral duty to other people prompt him to act.

The manager asks Joe to be careful to build their fire in the metal ring provided, and to thoroughly extinguish it before going to bed. Joe assures him that he has decades of experience with campfires.

"One more thing," the manager says. "If the wind picks up enough, I might ask you to put out the fire. I'm sorry for the inconvenience if that happens. It's looking good as far as the forecast, but I just wanted to give you a heads-up in case you want to cancel your reservation."

Joe smiles. "Makes sense to me. If it got too windy I'd put the fire out without being told."

"All right, then," the manager says. "Enjoy your stay."

As they set up the camp site and prepare to light the fire, Joe stops; he's not satisfied with the location of the fire ring. He walks to the office and finds the manager.

"The fire ring at our site is too close to the oak tree," Joe tells him. "I'm afraid some sparks might set the overhanging branches on fire. Do you mind if I move the ring a few feet?"

"Let me take a look."

At the camp site, Joe and the manager consider the situation.

The manager says, "I'm not sure it'd be far enough from those branches even if you moved it. I'd rather you used the ring in the camp site next door. You can move the RV to that site, if you want, or you can just use it; I don't have it booked."

"That's great, thanks," Joe says. "We'll just leave the rig where it is and move our chairs."

After the manager leaves, Sarah asks Joe what they decided.

"Looks like we got two camp sites for the price of one."

That night, Joe and his family get their fill of plump roasted hot dogs. He and his teenage son beat Sarah and his daughter in a game of charades, and as the fires die down around the RV park, Joe gazes at the stars and thanks God for many things, the blessings of liberty among them.

4

IF IT'S WRONG FOR CITIZENS, IT'S WRONG FOR THE GOVERNMENT

It is strangely absurd to suppose that a million of human beings collected together are not under the same moral laws which bind each of them separately.

— *Thomas Jefferson, 1816*

If it's morally wrong for an individual to do something, it doesn't become morally right just because many people decide to do it.

It is wrong to take your money by force and give it to someone else. Just because a majority decides to do it doesn't make it right, yet we have tax-funded welfare.

It is wrong to defraud people with Ponzi schemes. Just because the government does it doesn't make it right, yet we have the grossly misnamed "social security" program.

I have no right to force you to buy health insurance. Just because the government requires you to doesn't make it right, yet we have Obamacare.

You have no right to force a dairy to pasteurize the milk they sell. Just because the government tells them to doesn't give it the right, yet we have the FDA and all their food processing rules.

You have no right to take my money to pay for the education of your children. Just because the state decides to do it doesn't make it right, yet we have government schools funded by taxes.

You have no right to pass off fraudulent money – it's called counterfeiting. Just because the government decides to do it doesn't make it right, yet we have the Federal Reserve and "fractional reserve banking," which is just a euphemism for counterfeiting.

In all these situations, the state is doing something that would be illegal if it were done by you or me. We've gotten used to the idea that the state has this privilege, but I urge you to question the basis for this. Are you used to it only because it's the way we've done it for a long time?

In reality, there is no separate entity out there called "the state." It's not a thing with a personality, or rights, or obligations, or a conscience, or any of those characteristics we associate with a person. It's just a label attached to a group of people, like "the Steelers" or "the ham radio club." The state is nothing without the people who are in that particular club.

The people who work for the state are like you and me; human beings who eat, sleep, and breathe. A police officer is just another guy; if he didn't wear a uniform or a molded piece of metal we call a badge, you wouldn't accord him any special rank or privilege.

Some people in government don't wear badges or special uniforms, but they claim very special privileges too. There are fortified bunkers in several places across the country.

These "doomsday shelters" are deep underground, stocked with years of provisions, well-defended with weapons and high-tech security systems, and they are paid for by us, the taxpayers. But should a doomsday event occur, the ones who paid for these shelters are not the ones allowed to enter them – only a few privileged individuals are allowed; our rulers.

Look how our elected officials travel. The Speaker of the House of Representatives has military aircraft at her disposal, and she treats it like a royal perk. During 2008 and 2009, the Speaker's travels cost the taxpayers more than $2 million, including over $100,000 for alcoholic beverages.[12] Imagine spending over $4000 a month on mixed drinks. Why are we paying for this? Is it because we want to, or because they force us to? Even if some people are willing to pay for this extravagance, there are many who are not willing. Forcing them to pay is wrong.

If spending $2 million for Nancy Pelosi's two years of travel bothers you, you're not going to like the cost of President Obama's December 2010 Hawaiian vacation; nearly $1.5 million, not including several cost items that the government refused to disclose.[13] It would take the average American about twenty years of income to pay for that. The people in government who enjoy these privileges are often the ones who complain loudly about "corporate corruption" and "unconscionable CEO compensation." The politicians then

---

12 See Judicial Watch Press Release, "Judicial Watch Uncovers New Documents Detailing Pelosi's Use of Air Force Aircraft," Jan. 28, 2010 (http://www.judicialwatch. org/news/2010/jan/judicial-watch-uncovers-new-documents-detailing-pelosis-use-air-force-aircraft).

13 Marc Tapscott, "President and family on multi-million dollar Christmas vacation in Hawaii," *The Washington Examiner*, Dec. 29, 2010 (http://washingtonexaminer.com/ blogs/beltway-confidential/2010/12/president-and-family-multi-million-dollar-christmas-vacation-hawa). Obama and the 111th Congress are not the first to abuse the taxpayer's money – that has been going on for a long time. They're just more brazen about it now, because the public is numb, and government spending has become a juggernaut.

hold hearings and summon the CEOs to testify, making them justify their private-sector compensation. Since corporate productivity is in part what generates the tax money the politicians waste, they're the ones who should be called on the carpet.

Politicians do the very things they complain about citizens doing, except it's even worse because the politicians take our money by force before wasting it, whereas the big corporation has obtained our money in a voluntary transaction. I wanted to buy some groceries at Wal-Mart, and was happy to pay their low prices. If you don't like how much Wal-Mart pays its CEO, shop elsewhere. But if you don't like your government, you don't have another one to choose from.

There's an upside-down moral standard for the state. Its agents live by rules they forbid us to live by. They exercise privileges they won't let us have. Somehow we have gotten used to the idea that government people should be allowed to do things that citizens are punished for. If you're comfortable with this idea, you have played into their hands; the state needs most people to consent to its rule.

5

MONOPOLIES AND THE STATE

You were probably taught that the only thing that stands between you and gigantic monopolies is a benevolent government. Like a lot of things taught in government schools, the exact opposite is true; monopolies only exist when the state grants a business a unique privilege – the privilege of eliminating all competition by force. In free markets, monopolies are impossible.

A monopoly is when a single company has total control of a market. For instance, if Zappem Corporation is the only entity with the right to distribute electricity in your area, it has a monopoly. As you well know, your utility companies all have special protection against competition. If you ask why, they'll say it's because competition can't work in providing water or electricity.

This is obviously baloney. If it were true, they wouldn't need government protection to avoid competition; they could simply establish the business and the natural impossibility of competition would mean they had nothing to worry about. But you have never heard a utility say "Go ahead and compete; it won't work anyway, so our market is safe!" Instead, they run to politicians and beg them to carve out a monopoly for them like they did for the railroads. The railroad barons didn't get their wealth and power because of capitalism; they got it because politicians admitted them into the state's power structure. "Give us votes and we'll give you protection."

Monopolies only exist when backed by the threat of force. If you thumb your nose at the government and start a competing electrical utility, Zappem Corporation will get a court order and show up at your construction site with armed deputies. They'll tell you to stop selling electricity, and if you refuse they'll pile on top of you and beat you with sticks or even shoot you with a gun. Then they'll cuff you, squeeze the cuffs hard on your wrists, and put you in a concrete and metal cell. Zappem wins because of state-sanctioned force.

In a free market, the use of force to create or protect a monopoly is illegal. If Bob the Baker uses force to stop Frank Bunns from running a competing bakery, Frank can legitimately defend himself, and so the competition goes on. But when the state grants Bob a monopoly, it uses force to *protect the monopolist*. Thus, we see that in a free market the only legitimate use of force is that which is used to protect competition, whereas monopolies can exist only when the state uses force to sustain them.

When the state monopolizes an activity, it creates a particularly nefarious problem – political conflict. There is always a struggle to control the content of the state's product or service. Taxpayers resent subsidizing an activity they disagree with, so they strive to defeat their political opponents and gain the power to change the service to suit them. With government production of a service, the rule is always dominate or be dominated.

Compulsory public education is a clear example. Since we're forced to pay to educate everyone's children, and since our children are forced to go to school, there's always a fight over what the curriculum ought to be, whether it should contain sex education or not, whether it should be secular or religious, value-free or strictly graded, liberal or conservative, capitalistic or socialistic, integrated or segregated, and so on. Since the school bureaucrat doesn't have to sell his services in a free market, he doesn't have to respond to market demand, and so he chooses the path of least resistance by providing a uniform curriculum of general applicability, regardless of differences in the community. Moreover, he doesn't concern himself with efficiency or efficacy, and when parents complain about the poor quality of education his response is that he doesn't have enough money. Taxes rise, waste increases, the number of teachers increases, but the quality of education falls.

In a free market for schools, these issues do not cause social unrest. People educate their children however they choose, and if they're not happy with the school they change schools. If you want to focus on ethnic diversity, you send your child to a school that stresses ethnic diversity. If you want to stress Austrian economics, you send your child to a school that focuses on that. A free market responds to demand for diversity by providing diverse curricula; it responds to complaints of inefficiency by becoming more efficient; and it responds to complaints of inefficacy by doing a better job of educating. Otherwise it loses customers. The state doesn't lose many customers; most people will send their children to the public school, because they've already paid for it in taxes.

All of these factors leave parents with no choice but to join the fight to control the schools. This conflict is played out rather pointlessly in a contentious political process involving irate opponents and aloof, unresponsive bureaucrats. Even if they win the day and get some changes in the curriculum, they still live with waste and bad quality, from which there is no escape. And of course the losers are even more unhappy than the winners.

Another example of unrest due to state regulation is broadcast television. The Federal Communications Commission regulates broadcast TV, but not cable or satellite. Before the advent of cable and satellite TV, content was what you would expect from a state-created cartel;[14] bland and uniform across the networks. To increase their audience the network producers kept "pushing the envelope" of FCC regulations so they could air more interesting content, while the public pressured the agency either to keep the content family-friendly or to relax its prudish regulations, as the case may be. Then when unregulated cable came along, and later satellite transmission, programming responded to market demand – it became more diverse. We now have channels for weather, sports, historical programs, science, cartoons, faith healers, pornography, classic movies, Spanish soaps... virtually any conceivable topic. And the interesting thing is that no one gets up in arms about the content of these channels, because we don't have to pay for them via taxes and we don't have the state dictating the content. You watch what you want and flip the channel if you don't like it. You have choices.

The Transportation Security Administration is a dramatic example of how state production causes social

---

14 Cartel: A small group of individuals or companies with control of a market.

conflict. Under the pretext of making air travel safe, the government hires tens of thousands of agents, among them pedophiles and other sex offenders, who grope men, women, and children in ways that constitute sexual assault in any other context, and then responds to complaints by telling passengers their only alternative is not to fly. In this case, however, the conflict is not so much between various factions lobbying for their preferred regulations; no one is clamoring for more intrusive body searches. The conflict is one which frankly pits the government against the citizens, the rulers against the ruled. So in late 2010 there was a great, vocal popular protest against increasingly intrusive air travel security measures. It achieved nothing. In fact, the government doubled down, announcing plans to extend the same procedures to all modes of public transportation. The conflict heated to the point that the State of Texas considered a bill that would make it a felony for a TSA agent to conduct such a patdown unless he had probable cause to believe the traveler is carrying something illegal.

People want air travel security, of course, but that isn't the issue. The question is *how much?* At some point the intrusion on our liberties is worse than the risk of hijacking. Free people take risks like this all the time; the drive to the airport is far more dangerous than flying has ever been. The problem is that *it's impossible for the state to determine accurately how much security we need.* Security protocols involve not just dollar costs, but an assessment of the intangible values of liberty, safety, and chastity. There's no way to account for the value of these, which are strictly subjective and abstract, so no central planner can balance them when calculating how much security to provide. There's no chart that states the value of how badly Joe Traveler doesn't want to be touched in the groin so that this concern can be weighed against the odds that someone will hide a bomb in his underwear. As security measures become more intrusive, at what point does the traveler prefer to take the risk of terrorism on his flight? As he stands there facing the certainty that his wife will be groped, might he prefer to just tackle a would-be hijacker? If you asked him, he wouldn't be able to articulate a precise answer, and if he did, it might change tomorrow depending on what he read in the paper. And if you're the airline trying to please your customers with the least intrusive security measures, at what point do you feel compelled to insist on some amount of intrusion to protect your air crew and people on the ground, who are not involved in the security measures but who depend on them nonetheless?

These questions can never be answered, and they positively cannot be resolved by the state. Economics is a biological process with infinite variables. The economics of supply and demand can't be tabulated and codified for bureaucrats – they are too complex.

The amazing thing, though, is that there is a solution to these seemingly intractable problems. Almost miraculously, a free market solves them automatically. When air travel security is produced privately, producers and consumers (airlines and travelers) make these assessments on an ad hoc basis, and the quality, quantity, and market price of security reflect that assessment. No one person ever has to consciously determine the optimal amount or quality of security or the optimum price in any particular case – the security producer need only respond to demand. When the means of security production are publicly owned, this mechanism doesn't exist, and so it is impossible to optimize any of the value factors – in other words, you won't get the best security or the best liberty at any price, no matter how much you spend.

Unlike the capitalist producer of security, the government has no way to determine how much security is needed, so that becomes irrelevant. The government's only remaining incentive is to provide *ever more* security. Security production provides jobs for government agents. Government agents vote for the politicians who promise them more pay. Politicians therefore promise them more pay and more jobs. The politicians want more voters, so they tell the security providers to provide more security, and hire more security agents, who vote for the politicians. Taxes rise, security intrusions rise, and we lose liberty.

In the free market, the customer responds to bad service by getting service from a competing producer. When he gets bad service from the government his only recourse is to try to wrench control of the government from his political opponents. Again, it's either dominate or be dominated. This is an inescapable characteristic of government, and it applies to *everything* the government provides.

But as bad as that is, at least to this point we've been talking about what happens when the government provides a service we normally *want*. In the next chapter we'll see what happens when the state has a monopoly on crime.

6

CAN WE LIMIT GOVERNMENT?

A wise and frugal government, which shall restrain men from injuring one another, which shall leave them otherwise free to regulate their own pursuits of industry and improvement, and shall not take from the mouth of labor the bread it has earned. This is the sum of good government.

– Thomas Jefferson, 1801

The reason the founders created a federal government at all was only to prevent others from doing so, and their intention was to severely limit its power. Although they were the most powerful force for liberty in history, they assumed, based on the teachings of Locke and other libertarians, that government was unavoidable – a necessary evil – and so they held out for an ideal, constitutionally-limited government that would be a minor annoyance providing only that which government alone could provide, but nothing more.

The founders were bright, and their experiment in liberty has yielded wonderful dividends, but they were mistaken about limited government. Once you understand what a government is, it becomes self-evident that it's impossible to limit government with a Constitution, which is, after all, nothing but a written document. A government is a group of people who have a monopoly right to tax. Taxation is enforced by the threat of violence by the state, which holds a monopoly right to use violence to enforce taxation. Citizens are forbidden to defend themselves against taxation.

With all this in view, now ask yourself: If we can't use force to stop the government from taxing, how will a mere piece of paper stop it from taxing? Once you give the government the legal right to use violence to enforce any tax, all written limitations are meaningless in the face of the state's guns. Understand that the government described in the US Constitution is a fantasy; a conceptual, intellectual thing that does not exist in the real world. "The government" that we deal with in reality is not some ideal, wise and benevolent entity, but a group of men with the same passions, faults, and lusts of the flesh characteristic of us all. The only meaningful difference between them and us is that they have the privilege of taking our money at gunpoint, but we can't do the same to them. Since they have the guns, the only limitation on their power is their respect for the Constitution and their own will to restrain themselves from using force we simply can't resist.[15] That's a slim reed on which to hang our liberty.

No matter how short the list of constitutional powers, the state has no real limitations. Even if the government's only constitutional mandate was to provide security from external attacks, the fact that this Utopian limited government had a monopoly on violence means that there would be no one

---

15 The fact that the guns and engines of war are in the hands of the citizens is the only thing that has restrained the state in Switzerland for more than seven centuries, and liberty is threatened even there, as the state chips inexorably away at the right of citizens to be armed. In the United States, the rise of totalitarian government is directly tied to the virtual death – at the hands of the state – of the Second Amendment.

else to resist its expansion.[16] Just picture the mafia, but worse because they have no competition and they do have an imprimatur[17] of legality.

Suppose that for awhile the government miraculously did perform only that single function defined in its constitution. As Murray Rothbard observes, there would still be the issue of how much of its service it should provide.[18] When a good or service is produced in a free market, demand for it determines how much of it should be supplied. The profit motive stops a producer from producing more than the market demands. But government services are not sold; they are produced and distributed with money taken from taxpayers under compulsion. There's no market limit to what government agents can produce, and more to the point, their only incentive is to produce forever more.

Government agents are net tax consumers; their wealth is directly related to how much tax they can take from the private sector. They have a monopoly on the act of exploiting people by taxing them, and as Professor Hans-Hermann Hoppe has said, "assuming no more than self-interest on the part of government agents, all governments must be expected to make use of this monopoly and exhibit a tendency toward increased exploitation."[19]

---

16 If it didn't have a monopoly it wouldn't be a government, but a private security force competing in a free market against other security producers, or else it would need to have a government to grant it a monopoly on violence, because the only way to sustain a monopoly on violence is by government-supplied violence. But this latter situation is a distinction without meaning; the monopolistic security force is subsumed in the government. Thus we see that government and monopolistic violence go hand in hand.

17 Imprimatur: Official sanction or approval.

18 Murray N. Rothbard, *The Ethics of Liberty*, (New York: New York University Press, 2002), 180.

19 Hans-Hermann Hoppe, *Democracy: The God That Failed* (New Brunswick: Transaction Publishers, 2001), 45.

Whatever goods or services a government provides, they are merely the excuse to tax. If the government supplies many goods and services it has many excuses to tax, but a single one will do. The government operates outside of the laws of economics, so there's no economic reason not to provide an unneeded amount of it. Since it has a monopoly on the legal use of violence to collect the tax, there's no institutional limitation either. No one can physically resist its production of unneeded, unwanted amounts of the service. The only limitation is whatever it can get away with politically.

A government with a monopoly on security production would provide as much security as it could get away with politically. It would forever increase spending, taxes, and deficits until the economy collapsed. It would secretly allow security crises to occur in order to frighten the public into accepting more security. It would even secretly cause security violations when necessary to obtain more public acceptance of increased security measures, as the Bureau of Alcohol, Tobacco, Firearms, and Explosives did in selling weapons to Mexican drug cartels, while complaining about the need for more gun control to prevent that very thing from happening.[20]

In order to expand the scope of its responsibilities, the government would expand the definition of security to include concepts we don't normally think of as "security." Food safety, clothing safety, construction safety, transportation safety, telephone safety, and so on; there's no end to the amount of safety you could provide if only given the task. The government would have multi-billion-dollar educational programs to teach children how to cross the street, how much

---

20 Read about Project Gunrunner. John Solomon, David Heath and Gordon Witkin, "Whistleblower Says Agents Strongly Objected to Risky Strategy," *Center For Public Integrity iWatch News*, March 4, 2011 (http://www.publicintegrity.org/articles/entry/2976/).

television to watch, or how to avoid dog bites. There would be a "textiles police force" patrolling the schools and inspecting what the kids were wearing to make sure their clothes didn't pose a health hazard. In a very real sense, healthcare is a matter of national security; the healthier the population, the better the army that can be conscripted to fight the government's wars. Under an ever-expanding definition, the government would assess any conceivable risk and regulate every human activity on the basis of its effect on "national security."[21]

In this way we see that there is no real difference between the kind of service the government provides and how *much* it provides. If you limit the kind of service, the government simply redefines services so that they fall under the one nominal constitutional power. What you eat, what your kids learn at school, and how much water you use all become a matter of national security, and under the pretense of providing a single service, the government ends up doing everything.

We would fare no better under a theoretically benign government with nothing more than a monopoly on the administration of justice; that is, a government that consisted only of a court system. Here we imagine ideal, impartial courts that settle disputes between citizens in order to prevent wild-west-style shootouts, and put criminals away to keep the public peace, but once again, the potential for totalitarian regulation of the population is essentially unlimited. For one

---

21 Just consider how the definition of "terrorism" has expanded in Western democracies since 2001. Today it includes, among many others, mere criticism of public officials (http://dir.groups.yahoo.com/group/LibertyStudents/message/1739); counterfeiting, see Federal Bureau of Investigation, Defendant Convicted of Minting His Own Currency, http://www.fbi.gov/charlotte/press-releases/2011/defendant-convicted-of-minting-his-own-currency (March 18, 2011); biker gang membership, see Nicholas Broadbent, "The Expanding Definition of 'Terrorist,'" *NewMatilda.com*, April 6, 2009 (http://newmatilda.com/2009/04/06/expanding-definition-terrorist); and violence against government officials, disruptive activities or threats thereof against computer networks, assassination or kidnapping with the intent to affect government policy (USA PATRIOT Act).

thing, "public peace" incorporates the concept of internal security, so whatever you can imagine in terms of the police power would come under the jurisdiction of the courts; just insert here our previous discussion about security production.

In addition to taxation, however, the judicial system profits from another social phenomenon – crime. The more crime you have, the more you need courts, administrators, clerks, support personnel, guards, offices, prisons, warehouses, computers, vehicles, judicial conventions, sentencing commissions, advisory boards... the list is endless. The more crime you have, the more fines the government collects and the more property it can seize. In order to keep the gravy train running, the government would have every incentive to increase criminality in the general population, either by increasing criminal activity or by defining ever new crimes from conduct that was previously non-criminal. There would follow a perpetually growing list of forbidden activities; the substances you ingest, the manner in which you travel, how much you pay employees and their working conditions, what you teach your children, how you develop your property, what kind of lightbulb or toilet you install in your home, how much you pollute, what you say about a judge or whether you carry a weapon within his vicinity, and what you import or export from the country. All these activities would be regulated under the single, limited grant of monopoly power to the government to do nothing more than administer justice, and our liberties would be in the same sorry state they're in today.

A Courts-Only government would lead to the creation of a massive welfare state exactly like the one we have. In the name of preventing crime it would turn its attention to social conditions; poverty, poor housing conditions, poor education, lack of healthcare, bad diets, and unemployment would be declared "crime factors" that had to be addressed. So we'd have social security, Medicare, medicaid, wage controls, the National Labor Relations Act, unemployment compensation, and every other destructive feature of the socialist-welfare state.

These programs subsidize the conduct that causes the conditions they address. That is, unemployment compensation subsidizes unemployment. Since you always get more of what you subsidize, the courts-only government benefits from a double-whammy; it taxes more in order to fund these programs, which cause more unemployment, poverty, drug use, and broken families, and therefore more of the crime from which it profits.

You'll find a similar situation no matter what single power you give the government in its One-Power Constitution. If all the government could do was build and maintain public highways, we'd have the most elaborate, expensive road system in history, and you'd never be out of sight of one. We'd have four-lane highways that had only one car per month. To create road-dependency it would be against the law to fly domestically, and as part of its highway-maintenance function the government would operate a single airline for international travel only. Highway security, of course, would be a principal concern of the government and threats to the public safety would lead us to the USA PATRIOT Act. Dumb drivers would be a hazard, so you'd have government schools to ensure good driving habits. Any conduct on the highways – including commerce – could be regulated. The government would erect an elaborate judicial system to deal with traffic infractions and violations of all the regulations. It would soon discover how to profit from crime the way the courts-only government did.

In the name of highway safety we'd still have the War on Drugs, public schools, and environmental regulation. A National Highway Traffic Safety Administration would expand its role to regulate any product that might be found in a car, including telephones (here comes the Federal Communications Commission), car seats (Product Safety Commission), hamburgers (Food and Drug Administration), and of course fuel (Environmental Protection Agency). The government would build roads all the way to the borders, then create a standing military force to keep invaders off of them. Soon this idle army would get interested in foreign conflicts, perhaps over imported road-building materials. Outlays would exceed revenues, and so you'd establish a central bank to inflate the money supply, and we'd have the Federal Reserve. Once again, the government would be as gigantic as the one we have today, all because we gave it a single constitutional power – the power to build and maintain roads.

Is there a natural law that dictates this result? Is there some property of the universe that forces governments to grow ever more oppressive? Everything I've just described is easily understood from common sense, from our knowledge of how people naturally respond to incentives. I don't have to *demonstrate* that a limited government would grow; I can prove it just by tracing out the events that lead to its growth.

Governments become ever more oppressive because it's the wicked option. If government were good it would protect liberty; because it is evil it violates liberty. It is not even sensible to expect a government to be good. Think about what government is; it's a group of people who have the privilege to take money from others by force and live off their production. This is simply theft, and thus a government's very foundation is crime. How can we expect such an institution to be anything *other* than corrupt, oppressive, and destructive?

There's not a lot of empirical evidence to show what it would be like to live in a society entirely without government. The history of the world is full of governments of all kinds, but they all have a common factor – a ruling class with the power to tax under threat of force. Whatever we say about governments, whether in favor of them or not, is colored by our experience with a government that has almost totalitarian regulatory control of our lives. Governments, even despotic ones, only endure with the consent of the governed, and one of the government's biggest tricks is indoctrinating people to believe that it is indispensable. If you have trouble imagining roads without government, it's because you've been conditioned to think it's impossible. But others have imagined it, researched it, and found private road systems to study.[22]

On the other hand, there is historical evidence of how supposedly limited governments perform, and it is obvious that they don't remain limited for long. It is indisputable that the limited American government established by the founders does not exist today. Maybe Thomas Jefferson was smarter than we are, but we have the benefit of hindsight and of over two hundred years of brain trust on the issue of liberty. Just as we've learned more physics and chemistry in the last two centuries, so have intellectual giants discovered principles of

---

22 On the cost and social benefits of road and highway privatization see Walter Block, *The Privatization of Roads and Highways*, (Auburn: Ludwig von Mises Institute, 2009). There have been many private road systems in the United States and other countries, and even today there are some private toll roads in operation. However, they face a competitive disadvantage against government subsidized roads; a taxpayer is already heavily invested in the public road and is, therefore, reluctant to pay an additional toll for road use.

liberty that Locke, Bastiat, and Jefferson had not learned. The limited constitutional government was a daring attempt, but clearly it didn't work. If we're going to restore our liberties and keep them, we're going to have to do it another way.

To many people, it seems as if I'm advocating anarchy, but that's not the case at all. What I advocate is that we eliminate the monopoly privilege of taxation and violence. I suggest we stop stealing money from one group of citizens and giving it to others while calling this activity "legitimate." In short, what I object to is institutionalized criminality.[23] If we abolish this and the result just happens to be that government vanishes, so be it.

I'm not for anarchy, at least not as the term is used by government employees who scoff at the thought of eliminating their jobs. I want to eliminate the criminal power of the state, and so statists call me an "anarchist." They use the word with contempt; in our political discourse the word has come to mean chaos and confusion, as if what I wanted was mob violence, riots, and mayhem. In that sense, I am certainly not an anarchist.

In fact, as we have seen, the state profits from some degree of chaos in society, at society's expense. To the extent that criminality benefits the government, it creates more crime. To be sure, criminality must not get to the point where the government can't dominate it, but a certain amount of disorder puts state-provided security in demand. Wherever that balance lies, it's the *state* that cultivates a certain amount of disorder and chaos.

---

23 Taxation is just institutional theft. That is, when we tax people, we take money from them against their will, by force. This is theft, by definition, but when we do it through government action, we pretend that it's legitimate.

The word "anarchy" originally referred to the political theory that a community is best organized by the voluntary cooperation of individuals, rather than by coercive government. The etymology[24] of the word "anarchy" is simply "without authoritarian rule." Individuals and associations of individuals, such as corporations, families, clans, churches, and civic organizations, are all that is needed in order to provide a peaceful community. They provide governance without government.

What statists advocate is authoritarian rule by a relatively few privileged individuals who don't have to live by the laws imposed on the rest of us; who take our money by force and provide services whether we want them or not; who hold for themselves a monopoly of violence to enforce their privilege of institutionalized theft; who ignore constitutional limitations on their power; who violate our liberties instead of defending them; and who destroy civilized society in order to profit from the chaos that ensues.

That's what I oppose, and if the only way to stop it is to eliminate all taxation, then so be it. If it means providing everything in the private sector, even justice, security, and welfare... great! We'll be far better off, and free to boot.

Change of this magnitude is frightening, certainly, but a little knowledge and understanding can allay your fears, so in the next few chapters we'll show how the private sector can do things we're used to having the state do, only much better.

---

24 Etymology: The origin and historical development of the meaning of words.

7

LIBERTY AND JUSTICE

In the natural order of creation, the application of law is the process of determining the objectively just state of affairs in the relationship between human beings. It is a search for (a discovery of) justice, and it is understood to apply to all men equally regardless of their position in the social hierarchy. That is, the prohibition against theft would apply the same to everyone, regardless of his race, religion, wealth, or other social classification. This is called natural law.

In democratic societies the law is a very different thing. It is not discovered, it is made by those who have political power for the moment, and instead of applying the same rules to everyone, it is used to create privileges or penalties for various social groups. This is what we call political law or legislative law.

Thus, providers of certain services like electricity are granted monopolies; landlords are forced to retain certain tenants at below-market rates; employers are forced to provide above-market wages; union members are granted a degree of immunity for committing violent crimes; government officials are granted the privilege of taking the property of private citizens with impunity; doctors are authorized to assault people in the name of providing unwanted medical care; money is forcibly taken from one class of citizens and given to another; specific segments of the population are granted favored status in university admissions; "victims" of every kind are legally defined and granted privileged status.

This legislative victimization has another bad consequence; political law (a.k.a. "legislation") creates unnatural social inequalities. There are natural inequalities; exceptional athletes, brilliant intellectuals, fabulously rich businessmen, noble patriarchs, and so on, in contrast with sickly, handicapped individuals, people of low intelligence, unwise investors, and violent brutes unfit for parenting. The inequalities created by political law – instead of by the naturally-occurring activities of people in a free society – cause unnatural and dysfunctional social tensions. In an ideal free society with voluntary submission to governance, it is the most intelligent and noble citizen who will rise to the position of judge, advisor, or influential "village elder," and he will dispense justice, wisdom, and good sense. In a society of political laws which rule over and dominate the citizens, it is the most successful trickster, liar, conman, and demagogue who rises to the top. You can't expect this person to govern well.

In every way, political laws are harmful to our society, and yet, in our system, the courts are bound to apply them, and so the court system itself if disconnected from justice. While cloaked in a pretense of legitimacy by virtue of the fact that it occurs by democratic majority rule, the laws created by legislation are whimsical, totalitarian in scope and application, and have no relation to universal, objective principles of justice. Judicial production declines in quality, and therefore declines in its perceived value. As it declines in value, people begin to hold it in lower esteem; eventually there is a widespread contempt for law in general. Because it is unpredictable, it causes uncertainty in the way people order their affairs, so they become more short-sighted and less future-oriented. Savings rates decline, capital formation and investment decline, interest rates rise, planning, patience, civility, caution, wisdom, productivity, charity, generosity, tolerance, and hospitality all decline. Crime, parasitism, waste, recklessness, and delinquency all rise.

Meanwhile, since the legal system has become incompetent to do real justice, just results have become scarce, but the demand for them remains high, and so the price of real justice has risen dramatically. Getting a just result in court has become difficult and expensive. All this because politicians have taken on the job of making law, instead of leaving to judges the task of discovering it.

This problem can't be solved by electing the "right" candidates or appointing the "right" judges, because the problem is not cultural or political, it is systemic. It is not a matter of ideology, but of the inescapable laws of economics. Because of the way our government is constructed, this degradation of the judiciary is inevitable, no matter who's in charge.

The root of the problem is that the government has a monopoly on the administration of justice. Whenever a producer is a monopolist, he will maximize cost and minimize value. The government court system is simply a monopolistic producer of judicial administration.

Let's consider the government's performance as a criminal justice system. From the get-go we have a problem. To have an entity (the state) whose very existence is based in criminality (systematic theft by taxation and counterfeiting) in charge of crime-fighting is contradictory, like putting thieves in charge of guarding the bank. Among other things, this ironic situation causes some criminals and law abiding citizens to be cynical and contemptuous of the government. It also facilitates corruption among government agents who themselves recognize the reality of their own criminality, and figure they might as well profit from it.

You can see the resulting poor quality of justice: we pay the state to prosecute a thief, defend him, and adjudicate the proceedings, then he pays the state a fine, and then we pay to feed, lodge, reform, educate, and entertain him. The victim gets little or nothing. This is not justice; it's a travesty. Clearly, the government is incompetent at administering justice.

Actually, it's even worse than incompetent. There are inescapable laws of economics that dictate that the problem of crime will actually be maximized by the government. That is, regulation of society by a government with monopolistic control of judicial administration inevitably increases criminality. The government profits from crime directly in the form of fines and confiscation of "crime-related property," and indirectly by increasing more public demand (and hence more tax revenues) for its services. Ironically, the war on drugs is actually a war to increase drug use.

The government has a number of tools at its disposal for increasing criminality. First, it can increase criminality simply by defining new crimes out of conduct that was previously permitted. Second, it can define "civil infractions" which are not technically crimes, but which result in civil fines and confiscation of property. Environmental regulation is an example which results in enormous amounts of revenue to the government. Finally, it can actually increase criminal behavior by subsidizing known risk factors of crime. For example, by paying out unemployment compensation benefits, the government directly subsidizes unemployment, which causes more unemployment, which is a known risk factor for criminal behavior. In fact, the entire welfare system rewards non-productivity, which has an overall decivilizing effect on society by increasing irresponsibility, dependency, rudeness, ingratitude, illegitimacy, divorce, single-parenthood, and in fact all the factors of dysfunctional families and communities.

There is a limit, of course, to how much crime the government can stimulate before suffering a political backlash, but as the public becomes used to it, and by sequestering much of the crime out of view in crime-ridden urban slums, the government can gradually increase the overall amount criminal behavior and raise ever-increasing tax revenues to deal with it. By demagoguery, the government can blame crime on the very social conditions it causes, and since criminals can vote (until they're convicted), it can tax even more money from the productive non-criminal private sector in a snow-balling transfer of wealth to the criminal elements of society. Even after conviction, they are housed, fed, clothed, and educated at public expense. Thus the criminals are subsidized, and then punished, and then subsidized again, all with your money. The government levies more fines, confiscates more property, and raises more taxes for welfare programs that cause more crime, which leads to more crime-fighting taxes; the government grows more and more powerful, and everyone's happy – except the good citizen.

We can see how this plays out, for example, in the war on drugs, one of the greatest mobilizations of the government's judicial and police power in history.

I don't use illegal drugs. I don't even drink alcohol. If I could, I would persuade everyone that using drugs and alcohol is a bad idea. My objection to the war on drugs lies in the loss of liberties it has cost me despite the fact that I don't use them. The drug users still use drugs, but my freedoms have been severely curtailed. Of all the social engineering items on the conservative agenda, the war on drugs is probably the most glaring failure.

It has cost billions of dollars, countless lives, and an alarming chunk of our liberties.

It has been a back-door for increasing gun-control.

It has turned law enforcement agencies into drug trade profiteers by passing laws allowing them to confiscate property even if the owner is never proven guilty of a drug crime.

It has led to the erosion of fourth and fifth amendment protections by constant pressure to be "tough on crime."

It has diverted billions of dollars to police agencies, strengthening their grip on citizens in general.

It has left untold numbers of farmers destitute as the US strong-arms other countries into destroying their livelihoods.[25]

It has led to corruption as government officials sanction or even engage in illegal drug trafficking for political purposes.

---

25 The US government pays to destroy crops grown by small farmers, and in every practical sense this policy *benefits* the drug traders. In Bolivia, Peru, Afghanistan, and other drug-farming countries, soldiers burst out of the woods and shoot farmers, burn houses, and destroy crops, all at the behest of the US. The drug traders welcome this practice; the demand for their product remains fixed, and the price of their stockpiles increases (especially with opiates, which have a shelf life of several years). The large traders move production to other areas and now control the production directly. The farmers who once realized capital gains now work the traders' farms as hired labor. The traders realize economies of scale and of vertical integration; their profits increase, but the small farmers suffer. See, e.g., Constance Garcia-Barrio, "U.S. War on Drugs in Colombia is Ravaging Farmers and Land," *Common Dreams*, March 26, 2001 (http://www.commondreams org/views01/0326-03.htm); Barnett R. Rubin and Omar Zakhilwal, "A War On Drugs, Or A War On Farmers?" *Wall Street Journal*, Jan. 11, 2005 (www.cic.nyu.edu/peacebuilding/oldpdfs/Farmers.pdf); Graham Gori, "War on drugs leaves poor Bolivian farmers hungry, desperate," *Miami Herald*, Aug. 31, 2003 (http://www.latinamericanstudies.org/bolivia/bolivia-drugs-03.htm).

Between 1920 and 2008 the US incarceration rate (the number of people in prison as a percentage of the population) has increased by 800%.[26] Since 1993 the incidence of violent crime has declined, but the rate of incarceration continued to rise.[27] It's hard to say why this is; it could be that criminals are committing an increasing number of non-violent crimes, or maybe they're committing the same number of non-violent crimes and we're just catching more of them.

But it's also possible that we've simply defined new crimes and are putting people in prison for conduct that wasn't previously illegal. This has happened before, with Prohibition. The 18th Amendment was passed in 1919, banning the sale of alcohol, and within five years the prison population had doubled.

As far as I can tell, the USA has the highest documented incarceration rate in the world. Of course, there might well be countries with a higher rate, and they just don't publish their rates like we do, but it's still tragic that the United States, supposedly the world's beacon of liberty, should have so many of its own citizens in prison.

Clearly something is wrong. In every respect, the War on Drugs has been a failure.

If the purpose of the War on Drugs was to eliminate the drug trade, it hasn't even come close. The use of illegal drugs has increased steadily at least since 1979.[28]

One of the favorite arguments for banning drugs is that it harms the user, so banning them will improve his life. But it's no one's business whether a man harms himself – if it is,

---

26 Wikipedia, *War On Drugs*, (http://en.wikipedia.org/wiki/War_on_Drugs).

27 Wikipedia, *Incarceration In The United States*, (http://en.wikipedia.org/wiki/Incarceration_in_the_United_States).

28 Office of National Drug Control Policy, *Drug Use Trends*, http://www.whitehousedrugpolicy.gov/publications/factsht/druguse/ (October 2002).

it means we have a property right in his body; and if that's the case there's nothing to stop us from telling him he can't eat candy, can't watch TV, and can't lay out in the sun, and that he must eat organic spinach, must go to church, and must exercise, all for his own good. For that matter, if we own his body, why not frankly enslave him and put him to work for us?

Anyway, most convicted drug users keep using drugs after they "do their time," so all that has been accomplished is to turn them into convicted criminals with fewer job opportunities, less experience mingling in the community, and a stalled education. Didn't do him much good, did it?

Another pet argument for criminalizing drug use is that drug use leads to crime. It sounds pretty convincing at first, but this argument is actually an object lesson in how we should be skeptical any time we hear an argument that expands the power of the state, because criminalizing drug use makes the problem much worse rather than solving it. The truth is that if drug use leads to crime in order to finance the habit, criminalizing the habit will lead the drug user to commit crimes even *more*. The very fact of criminalizing drugs and of reducing their supply *increases* the price of drugs. The drug user who runs out of money will be driven to crime to satisfy his drug appetite, and making the drug use itself criminal will do this much more.

Another way to see that this argument doesn't hold water is to understand that the causal connection between drug use and crime also exists between any appetite and crime. The man driven to desire something powerfully enough will commit a crime to satisfy it. Even the prophet Agur recognized that he would steal if hungry enough:

Two things have I required of thee; deny me them not before I die: Remove far from me vanity and lies: give me neither poverty nor riches; feed me with food convenient for me: Lest I be full, and deny thee, and say, Who is the LORD? or lest I be poor, and steal, and take the name of my God in vain.

– Proverbs 30:7-9 (emphasis added)

Like drug use, hunger also leads to crime, but Agur's wise solution was to pray for an abundance of food. If you want to reduce drug-related crime, let the market provide an abundance of drugs. Just ask yourself: is the drug crime problem better now than it was a century ago, before drugs were illegal?

By decriminalizing drugs you're not approving their use. You can deal with it on a personal level much more effectively than the way it's being handled now. If you disapprove of someone using drugs, handle the situation the same way you handle any reprobate. How do you deal with a liar, a scoundrel, a philanderer, or a drunk? You can always fire the drug user who works for you; discriminate against businesses that have a lax drug use policy; and ban drug users from your church, house, or civic club.

———— ∽◌∾ ————

There is a lot of information on the Internet about the war on drugs, but you don't have to get specific numbers to understand its complete failure. All you have to do is realize that the entire punishment scheme for drug crimes hasn't accomplished any of the purposes of criminal punishment, which are retribution, deterrence, rehabilitation, and incapacitation.

Retribution is vengeance, but vengeance is a personal matter, and the state is not a person. I don't know about you, but I don't get a lot of personal satisfaction knowing that drug users are staying at the Hotel de State. If I wanted vengeance, it just wouldn't be enough.

Deterrence is a measure of how effectively the punishment prevents the commission of the crime. Can we agree that since drug use has actually increased over the years, this is one big fail?

Rehabilitation is when you go into the system a loser and you come out a stable, productive member of the community. How often have you seen that happen?

Incapacitation is the one thing the system seems to accomplish in part. During the time the drug user is in prison, he mostly lacks the ability to continue using drugs, although an amount of drug use still manages to take place. It's like a game for the convicts, and a moonlighting business for the guards. But incapacitation is just temporary unless the criminal stays in prison the rest of his life.

So we can summarize the accomplishments of the criminal sentencing scheme for drug use and trafficking as follows:

Incapacitation – fail.

Retribution – fail.

Rehabilitation – fail.

Deterrence – epic fail.

The reason for this abject failure is a combination of things.

One is that it's just impossible to stop people from ingesting substances they want, whether it be food, plants, smoke, powders, liquids, or whatever. There's something deep in man's psyche that rebels at being forbidden to put whatever he wants into his own body. I have a friend in the rural South who never touches drugs, but as he puts it, "nothing makes me want to try crack so bad as the government telling me I can't." You might condemn his rebellious attitude in that it might cause him problems at some point, but it might also lead him to struggle for greater freedoms for all of us.

Another important reason our drug punishment policy hasn't worked is that the primary form of punishment is imprisonment. No criminal justice system based primarily on incarceration is ever going to work (although it is a very lucrative business for states and prison contractors).[29] If you want a model for a criminal justice system, look at the one established by God himself when he established the nation of Israel. There were four forms of punishment: Death, corporal punishment, restitution, and banishment of sorts, in the cities of refuge. Imprisonment did not exist. If it was an effective form of punishment, you'd think God would have used it.

We won't get into a complete study of the criminal laws of ancient Israel, but here are a few noteworthy points. There was no state to carry out the punishments or to levy fines – there were no fines. Restitution was very personal, to the point that if the criminal didn't have money to restore the victim, he had to work it off as a slave. Death was dealt, in some cases, by the Avenger of Blood. This was someone designated as the one who would slay a murderer on behalf of the victim's family.

Now, I'm not suggesting that we adopt the laws of ancient Israel; all I'm saying is that since our criminal justice system needs improvement, we might look to a better standard and learn a few things.

---

29 David DeGraw, "The 'War On Drugs' Is A $2.5 Trillion Racket: How Big Banks, Private Military Companies And The Prison Industry Cash In," *Real News Reporter,* July 10, 2011 (http://www.realnewsreporter.com/?p=6248).

———— ∞∞∞ ————

With a virtual government monopoly of judicial administration, our civil law system fares no better than the criminal system.[30] The USA's judicial system evolved from long experience with the Anglo-Saxon common law, which was a disciplined process for discovering justice in any given situation. Unfortunately, this quest for justice has been nearly abolished and replaced with a system of codified laws; this has turned judges into mere clerks whose job is no longer to find justice, but to interpret statutory language.

Today the civil courts are clogged with claims, which not coincidentally benefits the government's judicial branch by increasing demand for more courts, judges, and administrators. The judiciary's budget always increases over the long term.

Lawyers benefit, of course. You need these experts who understand the complicated procedures, though not necessarily the law itself; the vast amounts of ever-changing laws make it very difficult to predict the outcome. Worse, the lawyers as a whole have given up trying to make sense of the impossibly complicated and contradictory legal system, and have cynically turned it into a cash machine. I have seen divorce lawyers all but openly collude to wring all the money they can from a marital estate. They set the husband and wife

---

30 The market for independent arbitration services provides partial relief from the government monopoly on civil judicial administration, but it suffers from serious flaws compared to a completely free market for judicial services. First, the government court is already subsidized by your taxes, so when you hire the arbitrator's services you're essentially paying twice for justice. Second, the arbitrator's rulings are not much better in quality than the government's, because even he is mostly bound to the laws produced by the government. Finally, as long as there are state-run courts, there will always be a demand for bad justice, because it can be used to obtain advantages unavailable in a good judicial system (e.g., one rich participant who can afford the proceedings vs. a poor one who can't), or just to torment a legal opponent out of vindictiveness. We wouldn't have this problem in a freely competitive market – in that system, both participants must consent to jurisdiction.

against each other, aggravating the conflict as long as they can bill their time, and then work out a settlement only after there's no money left.

The sheer volume of laws and regulations testifies to an absolute totalitarian regulation of everyone's conduct. The government has created an incomprehensible and contradictory maze of legislation that can't possibly settle the rights and responsibilities between citizens – they only create new conflicts. In this sort of legal environment, you can get sued for ridiculous reasons and lose your case. Thus we see that the civil law system also has become completely corrupt, for it is no longer a system for resolving disputes, but the opposite, a system for creating disputes as a weapon between citizens, corporations, and other social interests, with the result of creating a great and ever-increasing demand for the government's monopolistic production of judicial services.

A pervasive myth among statists is that to have justice, you must have a state to dispense it. In fact, the opposite is true; the state impedes the administration of justice and, if the state grows powerful enough, it eventually corrupts justice completely.

It's easy to see that the state is unnecessary for providing justice once you understand that justice is a relational issue between persons, and the existence of the state is irrelevant in determining the nature of the relationship between those persons. If I steal from you, I've done you harm whether the state exists or not. If I murder someone, we determine his vital status without reference to the state, and an eyewitness to the murder judges the circumstances in his own mind, based on his own experience. In fact, my own conscience judges my actions, and the state is irrelevant in that calculus.

But suppose the eyewitness and I disagree about my guilt; he says I murdered the victim, but I say the eyewitness turned and looked too late to see that I was merely defending myself. There is a process for determining the truth of the matter, and in our judicial system that process used to be called the "common law" system.

Common law is a process of discovering objective, universal principles of right and wrong. It is based on the idea that just as there are universal physical laws, so are there universal moral laws. In the physical world, you can observe the behavior of objects and discover universal laws of motion, as Newton did. In the same way, you can observe the behavior of people and discover principles of right and wrong.

American courts applied these principles until just a few decades ago. They were learned during several centuries of experience in the English common law system. We have accumulated a great deal of scientific knowledge in the last two centuries; in the same way, our courts became experts at discovering right and wrong. The laws were predictable, stable, and easily articulated; as a result, social interactions of every kind were well-defined. You could run a business with confidence that your contracts were enforceable. Prosperity abounded.

In the common law system, courts assume that right and wrong are objectively out there in the universe, waiting to be discovered. As each case comes up, the courts examine the facts and the dispute between the parties, and attempt to discover the one objectively right outcome. In other words, the job of the courts was to do justice.

The American political philosophy revived an important legal principle from the Middle Ages. It was the idea that because these principles of right and wrong are universal, they apply to governments just as they do to individuals. For this reason, common law was a check on the power of government, and individuals had little to fear from it.

This is no longer the way things are done. What we have now is legislative law.

Legislative (or political) law is the codification of principles created by man, subject to his whim, informed by the most pressing political pressures of the moment. What is legal today might be illegal tomorrow, dictated by whichever politicians happen to be in power at the moment.

This has a devastating impact on our economy because people can't invest in a business and have any confidence that their predictions are accurate; they can't have confidence that their investment will pay off. It's perfectly legal to build a shopping center today, but what if it's illegal in six months because some sort of rare plant lives on the property you're thinking about buying and developing?

Steve Wynn is a multi-billionaire widely credited with the economic boom in Las Vegas during the late twentieth century. Consider what he has to say when asked why he's moving half his business to China:

"Macau has been steady. The shocking, unexpected government is the one in Washington. That's where we get surprises every day. That's where taxes are changed every five minutes. That's where you don't know what to expect tomorrow. To compare political stability and predictability in China to Washington is like comparing Mt. Everest to an ant hill. Macau and China is stable. Washington is not.

Is there a businessman or a media person in America that isn't frightened about the next crazy idea coming from Washington? The financial institutions, the cars, the businessmen, the taxes, the healthcare... everything is cuckoo, and God knows what's next."[31]

You might find it hard to believe that communist China is a more favorable business environment than the United States, but billionaire Steve Wynn thinks so, and he says it's because of all the changing laws that come out of Washington. At least in China the communists have decided to make laws favorable to business.

I'm not suggesting that a communist government is good for us. On the contrary, it's just as bad for our liberties as the US government. But what Steve Wynn has found is that since the communist Chinese government is not subject to political pressure, they can make the laws however they choose and keep them stable. It so happens that they have chosen to make the laws favorable for business.

I'm not willing to exchange liberty for stability. Fortunately, we can have both. There is a way to preserve liberty and have a stable business environment.

The problem for American business is the instability caused by excessive, unconstitutional government power. The solution is to deprive Washington of the power to pass all these ever-changing laws and return to a common law system which is based on the stable, universal principles of right and wrong.

Like anything else, getting good at doing justice takes practice, and our courts are out of practice. It may take some time for judges and lawyers to get good again at discovering justice, but they should get started right away. In time, they'll

---

31 Jane Wells, "Steve Wynn Takes on Washington, Vegas & EBITDA," *CNBC News,* May 28, 2010 (http://www.cnbc.com/id/37392344/Steve_Wynn_Takes_on_Washington_ Vegas_EBITDA) Watch the video at http://www.truthaboutliberty.com/economics/steve-wynn-on-the-economy/.

relearn what they've forgotten and start resolving difficult issues as they arise in business and culture.

Then we'll have a stable business environment.

One of the great advantages of a common law system is that its regulation of conduct is extremely specific to a particular harm. For example, imagine a free country (yes, imagine that!) in which there are no zoning laws. Someone buys a piece of land next to yours in a residential neighborhood and proceeds to build a fireworks factory. He builds a storage shed ten feet from your bedroom in which he stores explosives and stinky chemicals. In this hypothetical free country you can't appeal to a zoning board, because it doesn't exist; you have to file a nuisance claim in court.

A claim at common law is a legal process that examines very specific competing interests – in this case, it's your safety and well-being versus his business interests – and crafts a very specific remedy. In this case, a court would probably stop your new neighbor from conducting that particular business on that particular property.

It makes sense, right? You were there first; it's a residential neighborhood; and the smelly chemicals and explosives pose a nuisance and an unreasonable risk to the residents. If your neighbor wants to make fireworks, he'll have to do it where it won't bother everyone in the neighborhood. This result strikes you as being just "good common sense," which is characteristic of common law systems.

And notice how this very specific case influences other people in the community even without imposing restrictions on everyone. In the future, a prospective property-buyer will examine the court's decision and self-regulate his conduct. He'll learn the principles of justice the court applied in the previous case and apply them to his own situation. If he's going to build a hog-raising operation, he might choose to buy property outside of town, or if in doubt he might even ask the neighbors how they feel about the business so he can determine if it will be a nuisance. If he's going to build a basket weaving business, he won't hesitate to buy the property.

Contrast this with a political law system of written, codified rules of conduct, which has general application to the entire population. By its very nature it is the opposite of specific, and people get snared in regulations the law was never meant to apply. The use of "common sense" is important in common law systems, but irrelevant in political law systems like ours, and so general laws often have absurd consequences.

Consider the case of Ashley Smithwick of Sanford, North Carolina.[32] She was a Senior in high school, played on the soccer team, and took college-level courses. One day, she and her dad got their lunch boxes mixed up, and the school just happened to do a random drug search. When they opened her lunch box, they found a small paring knife that her dad used for cutting his apple. Although she's never been in trouble, she was suspended from school for the rest of the year and charged with a crime. The Superintendent's explanation for this draconian decision is this: "We want to ensure every child feels safe on our campus."

Safe from what? There was no evidence that Ashley posed any threat. If the mere presence of a paring knife makes a child feel unsafe, should they be allowed back home where the parents hoard a whole cutlery set or, God forbid, a gun?

---

32 Bryan Mims, "Lunchbox mix-up leads to charges for Sanford student," *WRAL.com*, Dec. 28, 2010 (http://www.wral.com/news/local/story/8845676/).

This isn't the worst of it. As I mentioned, no one has claimed that Ashley posed any kind of threat, but this is irrelevant in a world governed by political law, and even citizens have gotten used to this. Here's a comment on the web site that posted the article: "The rules may be draconian, but they exist and the principal must issue the same consequences for all students."

Really? The presence of a knife must incur the same consequence "for all students?" I know a lot of you are saying "yes," but I ask you, why? Why is it not relevant that Ashley was no threat to anyone? Why is it irrelevant that she did no one any harm? Why must she be punished for unknowingly possessing an object? If someone put a sign on your back without your knowledge that said "kick me," would you think it was fair when people started kicking you? Would you just accept the presence of the sign as an explanation?

What if you accidentally put on someone else's coat and then got arrested for possession of cocaine; would you just take your punishment without saying anything, or would you point out that it wasn't your coat?

You would certainly point out that it wasn't your coat, that it wasn't your cocaine, and that you shouldn't be punished for something you had no idea was even going on. It is manifestly unfair to do so. In other words, it is unjust to punish you in this case.

The same is true for Ashley Smithwick. This "zero tolerance" law is a political law of general application. It is manifestly unjust and unfair, and the result is absurd. This is characteristic of political law.

The idea that the rules must be enforced without any regard to common sense is the result of several generations of political law replacing common law. Like the person whose comment I quoted above, a lot of people have gotten used to absurdity as the new norm, and don't even suffer a jolt when asked to abandon good sense.

The specificity of common law has been replaced by the absurdity of political law. If the school principal had any common sense, he would have taken this approach instead: "It is against the rules to bring a knife to school for the purpose of going armed, but it seems you brought it by mistake, and didn't even know you had it. Just be more careful next time; put a big pink ribbon on your lunchbox and spare us the national press."

But the lack of common sense is the point here. Absurdity is the hallmark of political law. It looks like Robert Heinlein's adage is proving true: "Good sense is never common."

8

THE MYTH OF SOCIAL SECURITY

The social security/medicare/medicaid program (we'll call them all "social security" for short) was doomed to fail from its inception because it violates fundamental laws of economics; it is nothing more than a legalized Ponzi scheme.

Social security simply takes money from some taxpayers and gives it to others. As more and more people become eligible to receive social security benefits, the burden on the other taxpayers increases until there isn't enough money to pay them, and the system collapses.

It might give people a warm fuzzy feeling to know that they'll have a government handout when they retire, but they're stealing the future of millions of children. They get offended when I propose to stop their social security payments. I've heard them argue that they've paid their dues, they've planned their financial future with Social Security income in mind, and now they want their benefits. Well, they should have known better. We told them all along that it was unsustainable, and that the government was wasting the so-called lockbox. They were simply taking other people's money, and what have they done to stop it? Our kids had no involvement in this whatsoever, yet they're going to be forced to send checks to people they've never met.

If your choice is between offending the baby boomers or stealing from your kids, you should prefer to offend the baby boomers. What's ironic about all this is that my proposal would actually make the baby boomers much richer than their social security benefits ever will. Lifting the crushing burden of the social security program would create an economic boom that would multiply wealth beyond anything we've seen in generations.

Social Security Destroys Society

Among "legitimate" functions of government (to exclude genocide, for example), social security programs are the single most destructive features of government in any civilization. All welfare systems are destructive this way, but social security is special because it is so gigantic. We'll see just how big in a moment, but for now let's understand how welfare is destructive; we need to know about time-preference.[33]

In economics, "time-preference" is a measure of how much an individual prefers to spend his money now instead of saving it for later. If he thinks it will benefit him more later than now, he has a low time-preference; he'll save money and accumulate wealth. If he thinks saving is pointless, he has a high time-preference; he'll spend now instead of saving and accumulating.

---

33 Government schools don't teach this kind of thing because if enough people were actually educated, they'd reject destructive government policies, thereby depriving politicians of the power they are addicted to. Private schools, including home schools, don't teach this stuff either, but only because the knowledge has been almost lost. Fortunately for our children, a few have retained this knowledge. Do your part and spread it as far and wide as possible.

Time-preference is a fundamental characteristic of socio-economics. It actually applies not just to money, but to goods of any kind and value, including abstract goods like kindness and generosity. A person with low time-preference is far-sighted in all ethical, social, and moral respects; he tends to be less inclined to criminality, drunkenness, or sloth, and he tends to have more children, a more stable marriage, better business relations, and more total wealth.

Low time-preference is good. It makes for a more responsible and productive society with high savings rates, greater wealth, higher and more equal standards of living, and lower crime.

High time-preference is bad. It leads to irresponsibility, low savings, low productivity, less available capital, squandering and waste of resources, moral degradation, and higher crime.

With that, we can understand how welfare programs like social security destroy civilization. Providing "public assistance" income to retired people reduces their incentive to produce their own future wealth, increasing their time-preference. In other words, they do less to provide for themselves, because they know it's just going to be given to them.

Moreover, a social security program increases the time-preference of those who have not yet become producers, further delaying their onset of productivity. That is, children, adolescents, and young adults know they will be heavily taxed to support retired free-loaders, so they have a reduced incentive to begin the hard work of earning income. Then when they finally do, they save less, because they know their future money is going to be confiscated and given to someone else.

The overall damage done to society is staggering. Economist Hans-Hermann Hoppe explains:

> *By relieving an individual of the task of having to provide for his own old age, the range and the temporal horizon of private provisionary action will be reduced. In particular, the value of marriage, family, and children will fall because they are less needed if one can fall back on "public" assistance. Indeed, since the onset of the democratic-republican age, all indicators of "family dysfunction" have exhibited a systematic upward tendency: the number of children has declined, the size of the endogenous population has stagnated or even fallen, and the rates of divorce, illegitimacy, single parenting, singledom, and abortion have risen. Moreover, personal-savings rates have begun to stagnate or even decline rather than rise proportionally or even over-proportionally with rising incomes.[34]*

All of this is caused by the increased time-preference that results when people look forward to getting their social security checks. In his book, Hoppe goes on to explain that there is also a relationship between high time-preference and crime because high time-preference (shortsightedness) discourages the virtues that are antithetical to crime, such as planning, patience, and sacrifice. It also leads to "personal recklessness, insensitivity, rudeness, unreliability, or untrustworthiness."[35]

I have just given you a philosophically precise way of saying what we've always known; welfare causes economic, cultural, moral, and ethical degradation. In other

---

34 Hans-Hermann Hoppe, *Democracy: The God that Failed*, (New Jersey: Transaction Publishers, 2001), p. 20, fn. 30.

35 Id. at 31, fn. 31.

words, it is socially regressive and destructive, which is exactly the opposite of what you've been taught. All wealth redistribution (social security, unemployment compensation, minimum wage, public utilities, public roads, any kind of market regulation) involves taking something from the one who produced it and giving it to someone who didn't. This reduces the incentive to be productive and increases the incentive to be a parasite.

As we have seen in our own country, this increases the number of parasites and reduces the number of producers. And since what we're taking from the producer and giving to the parasite is something "good" (otherwise it wouldn't be worth taking and the recipient wouldn't want it) this increases the number of bad people and reduces the number of good people. So we have increased ignorance, sloth, drunkenness, criminality, recklessness, and parasitism. Redistribution destroys civilized society.

That's why we have an increasing number of people demanding to take still more, justifying their own parasitism and encouraging it in others, and destroying productivity and private property rights.

Politicians redistribute wealth on purpose in order to get elected, and the people voting for them give the politicians the power to do it. If you support or advocate these welfare programs you are indirectly responsible for the ills in society you claim to be concerned about.

The Real Amount of Social Security Debt

You need to be aware of the concept of "unfunded federal obligations." This is the "fiscal gap," the difference between how much the government has promised and the tax revenue it has allocated to pay for it. In other words, the government collects social security taxes, but not enough to actually pay for all of the social security checks it's going to hand out. It's going to pay out more than it collects, and this is the "unfunded obligation" or "fiscal gap" of the federal government.

The amount of this gap is so huge that the government never speaks of it, because if it was too often on the public radar it would create very disgruntled masses. Boston University professor of economics Laurence Kotlikoff[36] has calculated the total unfunded federal financial obligations to be $202 trillion. Understand that this gargantuan sum is over and above the amount that we're already taxed to pay for these obligations. It represents more than four times the total net worth of all American citizens. Put another way, if the government confiscated all of everyone's assets, it would pay for only one-fourth of the unfunded obligation. It's over $670,000 per person in the US. If you have a family of seven, like me, then the government has saddled you with a debt of $4,690,000 in addition to your own debts and obligations.

Pause now and think about that for a moment.

Now, I know what you're thinking. You're wondering how the government's going to pay for this. The answer is, it won't. Social security is simply a legalized Ponzi scheme that has run for decades, and as we all know, these things always collapse. It's nothing new; governments have promised more than they could deliver during all the history of man, and the result is always the same.

There are only two possible outcomes; politicians will do the hard thing and renege on the promises, or they will do the

---

36 Laurence Kotlikoff, "U.S. Is Bankrupt and We Don't Even Know It: Laurence Kotlikoff," *Bloomberg News*, Aug. 10, 2010 (http://www.bloomberg.com/news/2010-08-11/u-s-is-bankrupt-and-we-don-t-even-know-commentary-by-laurence-kotlikoff.html). For a list of Dr. Kotlikoff's impressive credentials, see footnote 5.

easy thing and extend social security as long as they can — until it goes down in flames. The easy way means trimming benefits, raising taxes, printing money, or a combination of all three. Guess which one our politicians are going to do.

Any politician who points out how irresponsible this is will be accused of trying to starve your grandmother. He'll lose the next election and be replaced with another politician who will continue to promise money for your grandmother. They only live for the next election, and they will just keep putting off the inevitable as long as possible, hopefully after the next election.

By the way, this is why our constitution limits the power of the federal government. The founders knew that politicians will always take the easy way out, and they addressed this by providing that the federal government simply had no constitutional power to do anything except the 18 things listed in Article I Section 8. The federal social security program is absolutely unconstitutional.

There will come a day when we have no more social security program functioning. Don't rely on it for your future, because it's going to come apart one way or another. It may just bring down our whole economic system with it.

There is only one way out for us. We must elect people who will dismantle the system completely. This will require a huge power shift in Washington, and it will be resisted by those who stand to lose a tremendous amount of political power, but that is precisely the objective.

I realize that this will make some people uncomfortable, but it's better than the alternative, which is total collapse of the economy, in which case the program will disappear anyway. Sometimes saving the patient requires amputation of a gangrenous limb.

There are people currently receiving social security benefits. Many of these people have relied on the promise of this income in their latter years and haven't made other plans for their sustenance. In an early draft of this book, I had written a proposal to reimburse what people have paid into the system and stop the program, but even this is unfair. Who would pay the reimbursement? The money our parents have paid into the system has been squandered by the government. It's gone, and the nation is bankrupt. Sure, the payers have been defrauded, but to pay it back would mean stealing yet *more* money from a new batch of victims. There's no justice in that.

Let's illustrate it like this. Consider James, an elderly gentleman in Iowa, and Willy, a new college graduate fresh on the job market in Alabama. James has paid $10,000 in social security over the years, but the government has spent all that money. It's gone. Now we're ending the program; it's just going to go away. "Wait!" James says. "I was *promised* social security, and I paid in. Now you owe me!"

It sounds like a reasonable plea, but the question is, who is he talking to? He can't be talking to Willy, who just got a job in Alabama. Willy didn't promise him anything; they've never even met. So Willy can't be made to pay. I didn't promise him. My kids didn't promise him. Yours didn't either.

I suppose if you're going to hold the promissor to the promise, you'd have to go after the politicians who set up and perpetuated the social security system, but even if you did there wouldn't be enough money to go around.

So what's going on here? Are we to conclude that elderly James has just lost that $10,000? Unfortunately, yes. It was never more than a tax with a fancy name. James loses his money and assumes the risk of doing business with politicians. What did he expect?

The government was never capable of providing social security. People must provide for their own retirement. They must be allowed to accumulate wealth, and by the acquisition of wealth they can sustain themselves and their descendants. But to do this, we must abolish the income tax and the estate and gift tax as well, for they also deprive people of future wealth and increase time-preference. When income taxes are eliminated, it will cause an enormous jump in the net worth of individuals, and eliminating death taxes will allow people to pass on this wealth to later generations.

That's real social security.

9

THE STATE'S COUNTERFEIT MONEY

There is no subtler, or surer means of overturning the existing basis of society than to debase the currency. The process engages all the hidden forces of economic law on the side of destruction, and does it in a manner which only one man in a million is able to diagnose.

— John Maynard Keynes

The best way to destroy the capitalist system is to debase the currency.

— Nikolai Lenin

Our monetary system is designed in such a way that the government is able to carry out a slow, insidious degradation of the currency with hardly anyone noticing. Most people find it hard to believe that our own government would do this deliberately, but it's actually easy to understand why they do it, if you understand that inflation is the flip-side of taxation. The government inflates in order to impose an invisible tax on us.

Here's how it works. Let's suppose we start with $10,000 in the economy, held privately by people like you and your neighbor, and a loaf of bread costs $1. Now the government creates another $1000 out of thin air and spends it (see the section titled "The Federal Reserve," p. 97, for an explanation). Now there is a total of $11,000 in the economy, but no *value* has been added, so the value of each dollar drops about ten percent, and now it costs $1.10 to buy a loaf of bread. The government inflated the money supply, which caused the price of bread to rise. The trick for the government is that at the moment it spent its new money, its value hadn't fallen yet, so it got $1000 worth of goods for $1000. But by the time the money filtered down to people like you and me, we had to spend $1100 to get $1000 worth of goods. The government spends $1000, and the cost to us is $1100. Thus, inflating the money supply allows the government to tax us through the back door.

If you really want to understand how money works, buy the wonderful book by Richard J. Maybury, *Whatever Happened to Penny Candy?* It's like a whole economics course in 190 pages.

Worthless Paper Money

"Currency" is defined as the easiest legal means of exchange. For millennia, money was made from precious metals. A metal that has little value, like nickel or copper, is called a "base" metal. The practice of devaluing money by adding base metal to it is called "debasing."

A "coin" that has no precious metal in it is not really a coin; it is called a token.

What we use for money today in the US is completely debased, by definition. We use tokens and paper. Neither has any intrinsic value. So why does our money have value?

Because of a a legal fiction. Say you run up an account
with a feed store. You owe the guy $500 for horse feed. You
go to the store to settle your debt. You offer cash, but the guy
says "No way. That stuff is worthless paper. I only accept
gold or silver." Well, there's a federal law that says that if he
refuses your offer of US currency, the debt is canceled. So
he'd better accept it, or else. Thus, the government forces us
to accept a worthless means of exchange. The Constitution
authorizes the federal government to coin money, not to
establish a worthless paper money system. The founders
never meant for the government to destroy the capitalist
system by debasing the currency.

So how does this affect you? We have a monetary system
that is completely debased, and the consequence is the steady
erosion of the capitalist system. To understand how this
works, you need to know what phony money is, and what
capitalism is.

Capitalism is simply the voluntary exchange of one
privately-owned commodity for another. If I make rocking
chairs, and you're the Cracker Barrel chain of restaurants,
you want my rocking chairs for your customers to sit in and
play checkers while they wait for a table. You order 500
rocking chairs. I want your gold. So we willingly make a
deal – I'll make 500 rocking chairs, and you promise to pay
me however much gold we agree on.

But suppose we don't have a gold-based money system.
Instead, we use phony money. This is money that has no
inherent value. We only use it because the government will
punish us if we don't. Now the transaction is not really
voluntary; the only way I can participate in the economic
system is to accept payment with a piece of paper of uncertain
and ever-changing value.

Moreover — and this is the key — the money itself isn't privately owned. The paper is, but not the *money*. The piece of paper has no value. Even if you have in your hands a $100 bill, you don't own anything because there's nothing there to own. The value of it is entirely at the whim of the government, which makes it valuable in the transaction only by forcing us to use it as a medium of exchange. Phony money is not a commodity; it's a legal fiction. In short, the government owns all the money and controls its value. This injects the government into every single transaction in the economy, and this is the antithesis of capitalism.

You see, now the value of our transaction doesn't depend on the known value of the gold. It depends on how the government behaves, because it has a monopoly on money, and the money's value is subject to the behavior of corrupt government officials.

When we used gold for money, we knew the value of the transaction. But when we use phony money, the uncertain value of the money has made us depend on the government's behavior to make the transaction worthwhile. Now the value of the transaction is not controlled by the value of the commodity being exchanged, but by the political power of the government.

I mentioned that our current money system is the antithesis of capitalism, which is statism. Statism is the concentration of power in the state rather that in the individual. It takes many forms, such as socialism, communism, Nazism, dictatorships, and others. They all have one thing in common — they institutionalize the use of force against their citizens.

The Constitution authorizes the federal government to "coin" money and regulate the value thereof (Art. 1 sec. 8). This means to take a piece of precious metal of regulated weight and stamp it with a "hallmark," thus fixing its value.

And the Constitution prohibits the states from making anything but gold and silver coin a legal means of exchange (Art. 1 sec. 10). But our government bears little resemblance to its constitutionally authorized structure, and our federally-regulated educational system (also totally unconstitutional) doesn't teach the Constitution, because if the people knew what the Constitution really said, our government officials would lose a lot of power.

Power they aren't supposed to have.

The Federal Reserve

Our entire monetary system is based on a complete fantasy. It's a hoax, and we're the dupes. If anyone else did what our federal banking system does, he'd go to prison. Why? Because fractional reserve banking creates counterfeit money. The paper and base-metal tokens we use for money are essentially worthless, and one day there will be a jarring reality check.

Let me explain how the Fed works.

Suppose I need you to lend me $1 million. Suppose you're like most people and you don't have $1 million to lend. What you have instead is a magic spreadsheet. You can just sit at your desk and lend me $1 million that you don't have.

Now I've borrowed the million dollars, and I'm making installment payments, which include interest and principal. Over the next twenty years you collect about $3 million from me. Two million is interest, and you have to pay taxes on that as income. But the other million — this is the cool part — that's return of principal, so you don't pay taxes on that. Pretty swift, eh? Remember, you didn't actually have that million dollars to start with, and now you do, plus about another million after taxes, for a total of 2 million bucks free and clear. Not bad for someone who had nothing to start with.

That's how fractional reserve banking works. But there's something even more amazing than that. It's a very special bank, called the Federal Reserve (Fed). This is a private bank owned by a bunch of private citizens and corporations, most of whom are undisclosed to the public.

The special thing about the Fed is that it lends money to the government. Gargantuan amounts of money. When they lend this money, it comes out of the magic spreadsheet — the fed doesn't actually have the money to lend. It just invents it. Poof; there it is. But the government pays about $500 billion a year in interest on the national debt, and do you know where it comes from? Taxes. You pay it, and if you don't, you'll go to prison. We're all slaves.

That's why the Fed doesn't care whether the government ever pays off the principal of the national debt. The secret members of the Fed are sharing in an enormous amount of annual income, and they started with nothing anyway. The bigger the national debt, the more they earn. So there's absolutely no reason for them to demand payment of the principal.

History teaches us that systems like this always collapse eventually. The members of the Fed will come out on top at the expense of the entire economic system of the United States.

Just be ready.

Government Debt Steals Your Future

Like a lot of things, economics is not inherently difficult to understand — what's hard to understand is the complex stuff "experts" say when they're trying to fool you. When they speak, turn on your baloney detector.

The recent "economic stimulus" did not stimulate the economy, it only increased government power. Government stimulus has never worked, and never will, and it's very easy to understand why.

When we say the economy is growing, we're saying that the total amount of wealth is increasing. Wealth increases when people like you and me create things that other people want. We acquire greater wealth by making something or by providing a service that other people buy voluntarily.

The government acquires wealth by confiscating it from people who have it. There are two ways the government does this. One is by collecting taxes. The other is by increasing the money supply. You have to understand that when the government increases (inflates) the money supply, it is confiscating your wealth.

The government taxes now *and* in the future by deficit spending. Deficit spending is simply a future tax. Never mind anyone's fancy (and fanciful) explanations, when the government spends money it doesn't have, it confiscates your wealth.

Suppose you were the government. You want to spend two trillion dollars, but you're afraid to tax the people more than one trillion — otherwise, they won't vote for you. But you can't just spend one trillion — otherwise, they won't vote for you. So you have to spend the one trillion you taxed, plus another trillion dollars you borrowed.

Now, how will that borrowed money be paid off?

Anyone in his right mind understands that the extra trillion dollars will be paid off by taxing you (or your children) in the future. But it won't be just a trillion dollars. It'll be a trillion dollars plus interest. Plus whatever taxes you're already paying.

The government does this because it fears raising taxes enough to pay for all of its programs. It still wants to give you things you can't afford so you'll keep supporting the government. Ultimately, the government does all of this because you and other voters want it to. It will only stop doing it when the voters stop tolerating it.

In the history of the world, no nation has ever created more wealth for its citizens by spending tax money or by deficit spending. It has only reduced the wealth of its citizens while consolidating more political power for itself.

Anyone except a politician can see that this can't go on for long. Eventually the economy collapses. In fact, this has happened in every major economy in the history of the world.

You'd think people would learn.

Return to Commodity Money

We need a monetary system that has three conditions. First, it must be based on a valuable commodity such as gold or silver. Second, it must not permit fractional reserve banking, which is simply a politically-correct term for counterfeiting. Finally, no one, not even the government, must be allowed to have a monopoly on coining money. There must be a completely free market for money production.

In such a monetary system the value of your money would remain independent of political forces. The government would not be able to inflate, which decreases the value of your money. This is why every modern government has killed "gold-standard" monetary systems, and it's why we must return to a gold standard.

10

STATE CONTROL OF EDUCATION

The true center of correlation on the school subjects is not science, nor literature, nor history, nor geography, but the child's own social activities.

— John Dewey, founder of the American educational system

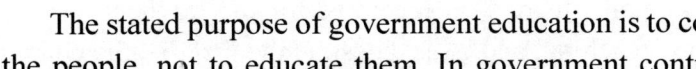

The stated purpose of government education is to control the people, not to educate them. In government controlled schools, the real instructional focus is on training children to be a part of society in the way that government fashions it.

People justify compulsory education by saying that it's necessary for the good of society, or that we all benefit when people are educated. But notice how the underlying assumption destroys individual liberty. The premise of compulsory education is that the state owns the child's mind and his future productivity. He's not a free individual; he's a slave owned by the state. Society is just a lot of individual human beings interacting with each other, but the statist turns it into a sort of collective being with the individuals as its servants, like the Borg in the *Star Trek* television series.

But whatever society might be, it has no right to this benefit in the first place. Even if it does benefit others for your children to be educated, that doesn't give them any right to the benefit. They're your children, not theirs, and they need to secure their own benefits by their own efforts. If it's wrong for one of them to take that benefit on his own, merely collecting a lot of people together to claim the benefit doesn't give them the right either; it just makes them a gang of thugs, or worse, slave-owners.

In any event, compulsory education yields less benefit than voluntary education. First, in compulsory education the students learn not what they need for their own good, but what they need to learn for the state's good, which is the essence of indoctrination. When the very thing that is good for the students – individual liberty – spells the death of the state, what do you expect they will learn?

Second, when compulsion guarantees that the school will have students, there's no incentive for the teachers to do a good job teaching, and indeed despite the fact that the United States spends more on its public schools than any nation in the world, we consistently rank below dozens of other countries in academic proficiency. In a competitive market, bad teachers are eliminated if they don't improve, but a state-controlled system eliminates good teachers because they make the bad teachers look bad; because they resist and expose inefficiency and corruption; because they put the children's interests above the state's; and because they are not rewarded for better performance.

And this brings us to the final point. The real purpose of government schools is to provide a gigantic pool of public money for a few privileged individuals to use as their personal stash. New Jersey, for example, has the highest per-student spending on public education, and the school system has "lost" many billions of dollars in recent years in administrative black holes, corrupt construction projects, and nepotism. The fearsome teacher's union has resisted every attempt to reform and improve education, to the manifest harm of the children. They use the students for their political and financial benefit; in other words, for money and power. Once again we see that the fundamental problem with state-run education is that it is in the hands of the state.

I recommend a documentary called *The Cartel*— it's a stunning exposé on the school system.[37]

Privatizing all education would resolve a host of intractable problems, such as school prayer. Our country was founded on Christian principles, but what if a majority of people in your community are Muslim? Would you be satisfied if they taught Islam in the schools? To avoid this issue, school boards have taken the position that they must avoid any religious content altogether, and the schools have become secularized. But this is no solution for people who believe that their children should learn everything in the context of their religious beliefs, instead of within the context of a secular humanist philosophy (which itself has all the hallmarks of a religious system anyway). It seems to be a problem with no solution, but in fact the solution is very simple. Just do away with government schools entirely and let everyone educate their children however they see fit.

Tyrants always seize control of education. By controlling education they control the context of learning and train

---

37 The Cartel, official web site (http://www.thecartelmovie.com/cgi-local/content. cgi?g=27).

children to toe the line, as it were, on issues that matter to the ruling class. The Thanksgiving holiday becomes a study in Pilgrim oppression of native Americans. Global warming becomes a scary fact and the children "must do something about it" (although in the 1970s the scary fact was the impending ice age – maybe they were too effective in preventing it). The earth becomes our master instead of a natural resource to be subdued and exploited. The spotted owl, the whale, and big trees become fanatical causes, while energy consumption and industry are personified as evil. The New Deal becomes our salvation, instead of the socialist disaster that it actually is.

So the children become political activists for the state, and meanwhile they don't know how to read, write, or calculate, and by no means do they learn to think critically about the issues in which they've been indoctrinated. The gargantuan sums of money we spend on education go not to learning, but to purchasing votes for our rulers in Washington, DC.[38]

You should have no doubt that the state attempts to turn your children into mindless, jack-booted conformists. Just consider some of the following measures taken in the schools:

Hand scanners to track students.[39]

Security cameras in bathrooms.[40]

Mandatory radio tracking devices given to students.[41]

A third-grader is nearly suspended for taking a two-inch plastic gun to school.[42]

---

38 By some estimates, Federal education spending in 2010 was nearly $160 billion. See, e.g., Christopher Chantrill, "US Federal Budget Analyst," *USGovernmentSpending.com*, (http://www.usgovernmentspending.com/education_budget_2011_2.html).

39 Steve Watson, "The Police State Takeover of Schools, *Alex Jones' Infowars.net*, July 24, 2007 (http://www.infowars.net/articles/july2007/240707Schools.htm).

40 Id.

41 Id.

42 Matthew Lysiak, Kate Nocera, and Larry McShane, "Laura Timoney fumes after son

A thirteen-year-old is required to remove an American flag from his bicycle because some of the other students might be offended.[43] None of this has anything to do with education. It's all about training the kids to be good subjects of the rulers in a police state.

Until we gain the political clout to abolish state-run schools, there is something you can do. Homeschool. The explosive growth of homeschooling in the last two decades is proof of how important freedom of education is to people who love liberty.[44]

Next to establishing a healthy relationship between the parents, the most important thing you can do for your children is to homeschool them, even if it means that one of the parents must quit a job. It's more important to give them a personal education than to provide the material goods you can supply with a second income. Those of the Christian or Jewish faiths will be interested to know that, whenever the Bible gives any guidance about educating children, it is almost always directed to the fathers, not a stranger, certainly not a government. Education is the responsibility of the parents, not the state. Don't think that you can compete with the state's indoctrination by trying to unbrainwash your child for an hour or so in the evenings. The state has several hours

Patrick, 9, is busted for bringing 2-inch-long toy gun to PS 52,) *New York Daily News*, Feb. 4, 2010 (http://www.nydailynews.com/ny_local/education/2010/02/04/2010-02-04_big_trouble_over_this_tiny_toy_mom_fuming_at_a_lack_of_common_sense_as_son_buste.html).

43 Elissa Harrington, "School Makes Boy Take American Flag Off Bike,) *KTXL Fox 40 News*, Nov. 12, 2010 (http://www.fox40.com/news/headlines/ktxl-americanflagbike11122010,0,3045879.htmlstory).

44 A 2008 study by the National Center for Education Statistics reports that about 1.5 million children were being homeschooled in the United States. http://www.nces.ed.gov/pubs2009/2009030.pcf.

a day, authority figures in the schools, billions of dollars to spend, and an irresistible mass of peer-pressure that it brings to bear on your child.

There's no doubt that it's a financial burden. Besides the lost income if one parent quits a job to teach at home, the family is already taxed to pay for the public education. The state won't reimburse that money if you choose to homeschool. But if you're genuinely concerned for your child, get him out of public school immediately.

11

STATE CONTROL OF HOUSING

A friend of mine (we'll call him Frank) wanted to build a house for his son and new daughter-in-law on his three-acre out-of-town property. They only needed a simple, small house, which was good because Frank couldn't afford much. Unfortunately, the government wouldn't let them build a small house – it had to be a larger house that met the minimum square-footage requirement for their neighborhood. They couldn't afford a larger house, so the newlyweds had to live in a room in Frank's house until they could afford to move to another town and rent an apartment.

Like a lot of today's government policies, these zoning laws had the effect of restricting the family's options and ultimately dividing them into smaller sub-units. If Frank's son and daughter-in-law were able to live next door, they could all rely on each other a lot more. They could share meals, provide babysitting, assist in simple household repairs, maybe help someone who is injured or sick, and so forth. Instead, this zoning policy required Frank's son to leave, and they are no longer as interdependent as they could be. Overall, zoning restrictions do more harm than good. They divide families and redistribute people into unnatural socioeconomic classes.

The typical justification for zoning laws is to protect property value or quality. In some cases I think they stumble upon a good result, as when someone might try to build a toxic waste treatment plant in a residential neighborhood, but even this could be handled by a public nuisance claim in a good common-law based judicial system. At least then the regulations would be specific to a particular harm, instead of imposing general restrictions on everyone regardless of whether any harm results. What if Frank built his son a really cute cabin that actually enhanced the value of the property? Never mind – it's against the rules, common sense be damned.

———∞∞∞———

I guess people generally don't want to hang out with people who are poorer than them. When I've asked why, the answer I usually get is that they don't want to live in a "bad neighborhood." They have come to believe that poverty causes bad character, and they don't want bad characters in their neighborhood.

Well, of course they don't; who would? But the idea that poor people are of bad moral character is pretty offensive, akin to the argument that "poverty breeds crime." By this perverse way of thinking, poorer people are somehow morally depraved and more inclined to criminal activity. This argument is itself a case of moral depravity; it is extremely offensive and has no basis in fact.

I would agree that bad character and criminal tendencies can lead to poverty, but it doesn't go the other way. If it did, then crime rates would have been much higher before the industrial revolution than they are today, but it's the other way around.

Growing up, I knew some people who lived in a house about the size of my living room. They kept a large garden and some farm animals, and I rarely saw them eat food they hadn't raised themselves, except for a few staples like flour, oil, and salt. These people had very little money, but the thought of committing a crime never crossed their mind. They were my grandparents.

And they were fairly well-to-do in their neighborhood. Others in the area were destitute by today's standards, but they never thought of themselves in that way. They lived in tiny houses without electricity or running water. These were very simple people with few changes of clothes and a simple diet. To them, a bent nail was an asset not to be discarded, and they had no criminal tendencies whatsoever.

People like them should not be banned from our neighborhoods. In fact, I'd rather have them for neighbors than people too snooty to talk to the likes of my grandparents. Most people welcome good neighbors, whatever the value of their house. In free societies it is common to see million-dollar homes right next door to small houses worth a tenth as much. Some highbrowed people live in neighborhoods with contractual restrictive covenants that set minimum standards for home values, but that's their business; at least it's not a law.

To this point, we've only discussed how the government regulates property you own; we haven't even mentioned the awful consequences of "public housing." I didn't have to observe the government-subsidized housing phenomenon for very long before concluding that it does more harm than homelessness.

The government provides housing assistance in two basic ways. One is project-based, in which poor tenants all live in the same building or building complex. Some entire neighborhoods are formed out of government housing. The other is a tenant-based system in which the government gives people a check that can be used as a rental payment for their house or apartment any place that accepts these checks – or vouchers – as payment. The first system consolidates poor people into a festering cesspool of criminal urban blight. The second at least gives the poor person the chance to shop around for an apartment in a better neighborhood.

Free housing attracts people who want stuff they don't have to earn. If you can have babies out of wedlock, have your medical bills paid by someone else, have your food, housing, utilities, and transportation paid by someone else, hey, what a bonanza!

Ken Rogulski filed a story that first aired on WJR news in Detroit, and audio of this story has been uploaded many times on YouTube and other Internet locations. It features two women who voted for Obama thinking they would receive free money from his "stash." It's pathetic to see human beings reduced to such a level, but I recommend you listen so you can acquaint yourself with the consequences of "free stuff" government policies.[45] If you support such policies, you should know what they're doing to people.

Sure, a few people are merely unfortunate and need temporary help on their way back up out of trouble. But mostly, the "free stuff" policies attract bad characters and turns entire city districts into crack dens. If you're looking for centers of criminal infestation and broken families, just look up your nearest government-subsidized housing project. And understand that these places are crime-ridden not because the residents are poor, but because government subsistence attracts and fosters the moral depravity that leads to criminal behavior. Poverty doesn't cause crime – the

---

45 James T. Harris, "Obama Stash," http://www.youtube.com/watch?v=_Ojd13kZlCA&feature=related (Oct. 15, 2009).

government does, all while perpetuating the poverty cycle it pretends to relieve.[46]

—— ⚭ ——

There is a persistent myth that a free market cannot provide housing for the poor. In fact, the very idea that poverty exists in a free market is itself a myth. There is essentially no such thing as poverty in free markets – poverty exists, if at all, only to the extent that the market is not free.

Even with all the hindrances and added costs of government suppression of the free market, in the past century, the US private sector has generated such phenomenal amounts of wealth that it has caused us to redefine "poverty." In the US, someone who lives in a warm, dry house and owns a car, refrigerator, washer, dryer, stove, microwave oven, TV, and DVD player can be called "poor." You've heard a million times that without Democrats to the rescue, the rich get richer and the poor get poorer. The truth is that in a free market economy the rich get richer and the poor get much richer.[47]

But when was the last time you heard that?

Back to housing. There's a reason why politicians provide public housing for "the poor," but it has nothing to do with their well-being. They are simply trading favors in exchange for votes.

The "poor" are not actually "poor;" they're just defined that way for political purposes. What they are is the recipients of political favors, and for those favors they grant political

46 Further reading: James Bailey Brislin, "Government Housing Programs Incubate Crime, Social Problem," *The Carpet City Chronicle*, Aug. 14, 2008 (http://carpetcity. wordpress.com/2008/08/14/goverment-housing-programs/); Tim Montgomerie, "A strong family and small state ought to go hand in hand," *The Telegraph*, March 17, 2009 (http://www.telegraph.co.uk/comment/5008047/A-strong-family-and-small-state-ought-to-go-hand-in-hand.html).

47 See, e.g., Don Mathews, "The Free Market: Lifting All Boats," *The Freeman*, April 1997 (http://www.thefreemanonline.org/featured/the-free-market-lifting-all-boats/).

power to politicians in the form of votes. They typically vote for Democrats because Democrats are the ones who promote the Marxist policies that benefit the "poor." These policies never vanish even during Republican administrations because while Republicans don't advance Marxist policies as aggressively as Democrats, they certainly do go along with them in order to get as much of the poor vote as they can.

Political ideology won't cure these evils – the only cure is to strip the politicians of the power to sell these favors for votes.

The whole business is a fiasco. The people aren't poor to begin with, so we're curing a problem that doesn't exist. To the extent it does exist (which is an extremely small extent), a free market and private charities would solve it much, much more effectively.

The politicians aren't helping the "poor," they're hurting them. Their so-called cure provides horrid living conditions, perpetuates poverty by discouraging self-help, destroys families, and destroys entire urban economies by creating crime-ridden neighborhoods that drive out businesses and productive, stable working families.

Whenever the government comes to help, you'll find carnage in its wake.

The subprime mortgage crisis of the late 2000s is a perfect illustration of the fact that politicians are completely incompetent to handle private-sector transactions. The collapse of the housing industry in the United States led to global depression-like economic circumstances from which we have still not recovered, and the cause of the problem was, from beginning to end, government intervention in the economy.

When a bank lends you money to buy a house, it takes a "mortgage" on the house. That is, if you don't pay back the loan, they can kick you out and sell the house to get their money back. The mortgage is the legal document that gives them the right to do this.

The bank typically doesn't keep your mortgage; they sell it to investors who like to buy mortgages at a discount. When the lender sells the mortgage to someone else who collects the borrower's monthly payments, this is called the "secondary mortgage market."

The biggest buyer in the secondary mortgage market is a government entity called Fannie Mae. It's just another business like Coca Cola or Ford Motor Company, except it's run by politicians and so it is rife with corruption.

As the biggest buyer of mortgages from banks, Fannie Mae had a lot of clout in dictating the terms of the transactions, and because it's run by a bunch of crooked politicians, Fannie Mae did a lot to corrupt the mortgage business in general.

At some time in the last century, politicians had the idea of buying some votes by providing "affordable housing," which meant forcing the banks to lend money to people who couldn't afford the payments. Fannie Mae, the biggest buyer of mortgages, told the banks they wouldn't buy their mortgages anymore unless they made these bad loans. So the banks lent money to people who couldn't pay it back, then bundled the bad mortgages with good ones and sold these mixed packages on the secondary mortgage market.

A lot of people who couldn't previously get a loan now lived in houses they still couldn't afford. They were happy for a short time, thanked their politician/rulers, and voted for more Democrats.

Meanwhile, Fannie Mae bought the bad loans. Eventually the people who couldn't afford the loans in the first place stopped paying, and Fannie Mae kicked them out and took their houses. Fannie Mae then put the houses up for sale. Suddenly there were lots of houses for sale, but not many people buying them, and the price of houses fell. Everyone's home values declined. Investors who had bought mortgages went bankrupt.

Fannie Mae went bankrupt and then your tax dollars were spent bailing out Fannie Mae and a lot of banks and insurance companies.

The politicians who had caused this problem in the first place blamed the banks and the insurance companies. Voters cheered their politicians because they thought the banks were the bad guys. The politicians passed new laws making the situation even worse, extending the economic pain – we got the bailouts, the "stimulus," and even more regulations like the ones that caused the problem in the first place. (Incidentally, the $768 billion price tag on the stimulus bill is pure fantasy. The true cost of the stimulus is at least $3.2 trillion.[48] Moreover, it's naive in the extreme to think this "stimulus" has improved the economy; taking that amount of money out of the economy so politicians can waste it doesn't help anything but to consolidate further political power).

As of mid-2011, the economy is in worse shape than ever. The only thing that has prevented total collapse is ignorance, due to the success of the government propaganda machine. If enough people knew the situation, everyone would get rid of their dollars, hyperinflation would result, and it would be over.

In any event, the cause of the problem from the beginning, and the cause of the continued worsening of the situation, is government interference in the housing market.

---

48 Conn Carroll, "True Cost of Stimulus: $3.27 Trillion," The Foundry, Feb. 12, 2009 (http://blog.heritage.org/2009/02/12/true-cost-of-stimulus-327-trillion/).

12

STATE CONTROL OF FOOD

To hear politicians, you'd think food producers only sell good food when the government forces them to. It boggles the mind, but abysmal stupidity of this kind is the underlying rationale for the Food and Drug Administration's authority to police what you eat.

I call it a "rationale" quite deliberately. Food safety is not the real reason for the government's control of food; it's just another excuse to tax and wield power. Politicians use this power to dispense favors, make threats, and secure personal gain – and also just to enjoy the rush they get out of exercising power. The power to subjugate others to your will and do things with impunity that are crimes when mere citizens do it, is apparently a drug-like experience. That's where the expression "drunk with power" comes from; the politicians are addicts, and we're the victims.

And make no mistake; the government does indeed police the food supply, with guns drawn. Watch this video, in which people in an organic food store are held at gun point while police search for raw milk: http://republicbroadcasting.org/?p=9870. There was no evidence that anyone was forced to drink raw milk against his will, or tricked into drinking raw milk thinking it was pasteurized, yet the sellers were treated like criminals, held at gunpoint, and had their goods confiscated.

If seeing this doesn't make you feel shock and outrage, please jump ahead to the chapter titled "*The Police State Mentality*," then come back and finish this chapter.

In a free market, food producers have a financial and moral incentive to provide the best possible food at the most reasonable prices. It is government that compromises the quality of the food supply. Government interference causes imbalances in the market. The government gives some food producers an unfair competitive advantage, and other food producers cut corners in response to the lopsided burden placed on them by the government.

The result is poor quality food. Government regulation caused the problem in the first place, but now the government points and shouts at the "failure of the unregulated market" and enacts more regulation, leading to more failure.

Once you set a precedent for government interference in the food supply, producers no longer attempt to compete in a free market – they go to the government to gain political advantages over their competitors. Once again, the problem is the government's power to interfere in the first place. If the government had no power to interfere, it wouldn't cause the safety problems and it wouldn't exacerbate them by distorting the market conditions that would, if left alone, provide safe, inexpensive food for consumers.

If you think I'm merely speculating or using hyperbole, just look at what happened during the 2010 lame duck congress[49] with the passage of the Food Safety Modernization

---

49 A Lame Duck session of Congress happens in even numbered years after the elections. Outgoing representatives (those who lost the election) are leaving anyway, so they don't care what the voters think about how they vote on legislation. Lame Duck sessions are particularly bad when the party in control loses the election; they're still in control of the congress and sometimes pass horrendous legislation in a fit of rage against the voters who ousted them. Lame Duck sessions became possible in 1933 with the

Act. This colossal legislative train wreck was passed when everyone was distracted with the Bush tax cut extensions, the new START treaty, and the repeal of Don't Ask Don't Tell. It grants sweeping new powers to the FDA to control the food supply. It allows the FDA to hire thousands of new government workers, and it is estimated that it will directly increase the federal budget by $1.4 billion over four years. The indirect costs are hard to figure, but they will be staggering.

To understand just what a boondoggle this legislation is, you need to understand the situation just before it was passed. For decades the government has been regulating food production and subsidizing[50] it at the same time. The government granted certain food producers special privileges that gave them an unfair advantage over some of their competitors. At the same time, the government regulations made it more difficult for new producers to come into the market to compete.

As usual, there was an unintended consequence; the very regulations that stifled the big producers' competition also made it difficult for the big producers to compete with new food market segments when they developed. We'll see this in a moment.

First, let's see specifically how the government affected food production.

The government heavily regulated the production of staples like corn, soybeans, and beef. Only gigantic corporations could bear the cost of these regulations and still make

---

passage of the 17th Amendment; as originally written, the Constitution did not allow for them.

50 A subsidy is a wealth transfer by the government to an industry or other economic sector that does not support itself. Welfare payments to individuals are subsidies of whatever economic factors resulted in the "poverty" the welfare payment is meant to alleviate. For example, unemployment compensation subsidizes unemployment. You always get more of whatever you subsidize, so this results in more unemployment.

money. Smaller producers could not come up with the capital to even start competing with them (which is to say that this market had very high "barriers to entry"), so they had little competition in the production of those goods.

At the same time, the government provided subsidies for the production of some of these goods in the form of tax incentives or even large government purchases, like the infamous corn/ethanol incentives. Since the giant corporations had most of the market for these subsidized goods, a disproportionate fraction of their profit (compared to the smaller producers) was attributable to political favoritism.

It's a bit complicated, but the upshot is that the government's regulations hurt the smaller producers more than the big ones, and the subsidies helped the large producers more than the little ones. And none of this had anything to do with free market forces, or the quality or safety of the products. It had everything to do with the government wielding power over the food supply, holding that power over the producers' heads, and then dispensing favor upon the highest bidder.

We can't discuss in this chapter all the factors you should study to really understand the economics of food production, but I'll explain this: Food production tends to have a low profit margin and very high fixed costs. That means that to get into the food production business you have to put up a lot of money to get started and expect it to take a long time to realize a profit. Got that? We'll come back to this in just a moment.

We left off at the point where the big food producers had onerous regulations and some offsetting subsidies from the government. But then a new market trend developed; people became more and more conscious of the benefits of natural foods, and became suspicious of industrial food production processes. All over the country consumers began demanding more wholesome foods, raw milk, raw honey, produce direct from the garden, food of every kind that was pesticide free, hormone free, unpasteurized, unhomogenized, organic, and natural.

Hippies became the neighborhood heroes. They'd been gardening since the 60s, and now they could actually earn a living with a legal crop. Vegetable stands sprung up everywhere. Farmer's markets boomed.

Pretty soon, organic farming became a small to medium-sized business; thousands of these operations flourished.

Remember what I said about high costs and low profits? Organic production is hands-on and labor intensive, and for this the consumer is willing to pay a premium, so that gives it a bigger profit margin. The giant producers could not compete. Their system is automated. It's a food factory, which is by definition what the consumer was avoiding. Their profit model depended on government-subsidized industrial production and government-stifled competition.

The only way high-capital, low-margin businesses can survive is in a competitive environment that is stable in the long term. Because the government had artificially suppressed competition for so long, the giant producers did not know how to respond when market pressures blew a competitive gasket in the natural foods market.

So they did what the government had trained them to do; they got the government to stifle the new competition. They demanded new legislation that would make it difficult for natural food producers to produce natural food.

The Food Safety Modernization Act of 2010 has nothing to do with food safety. Don't believe that for a second. If the purpose of the bill was to ensure food safety, they wouldn't have carved out an exception for operations that gross less than $500,000 annually. What does their gross have to do with food safety? The bill will not improve food safety or quality; it will worsen it, and increase its cost at the same time.

In fact, the increase in cost is deliberate. Remember one last time that food production has a small profit margin. In this business, a $500,000 gross revenue yields very little profit – there's little room to lower the price of wholesome foods, so the price will remain high compared to factory food. Without any doubt at all, the real purpose of this bill from hell is to increase the cost of producing wholesome food so that the consumer will keep buying the cheaper factory food produced by the corporations that had the favor of politicians.

A few die-hard good-food consumers will keep the small operations in business, but as the giant corporations (with their unfair government-sponsored advantage) slowly begin to compete in this market, they will eventually undercut these small producers, eliminate them as competition, and we'll be back where we started – with only regulated, subsidized factory food to choose from in the grocery.

Then the only good food you'll be able to get will be what you grow yourself. And as the case of Wickard v. Filburn[51] proved, the government can put a stop to that too, anytime it chooses. In this case, the government had granted only certain large farm operations the right to raise wheat crops; ordinary people like you and me were forbidden to. Farmer Filburn had a small wheat allotment – permission to grow a certain amount of wheat to feed his cattle – but he grew more than was allowed. When the government found out, they destroyed his crop and fined him. The US Supreme Court decided that was perfectly acceptable.

---

51 See Chapter 2: *The Kings of America.*

If our government paid any heed to the Constitution, we wouldn't be in this quagmire.

I know it's tempting to keep buying the cheap food. When you come across a five-pound package of hamburger in the grocery store and realize that your tax dollars have already paid for maybe a fifth or a quarter of it, you probably figure you might as well finish buying it and take it home. If so, I don't blame you. I've done it myself.

But understand this – cheap food is not cheap if it's bad for you. It's actually very expensive food in terms of the price you pay in being sick, diseased, or malnourished, and all the medical expenses that result. Once you see that, it's quite a relief to buy food with a higher price on the label, but knowing that what you eat is actually nourishing you in the way that nature's creator designed it to.

13

STATE CONTROL OF MARRIAGE

I have mentioned elsewhere that the state is a substitute for God, and the clearest indication of this is the state's control of marriage. Marriage is the very first religious institution, recorded in the book of Genesis. The government should have no more to say about marriage than it does about who should be baptized, or ordained as a priest, yet today you can't get married without the government's permission.

Make no mistake, today's assault on traditional marriage is purposeful, and the goal is ultimately to destroy the family unit.[52] The strategy is to do this incrementally so you hardly notice it. Today's statist government policies weaken families and make people more and more dependent upon the state, instead of allowing them to benefit from the security offered by a strong family.

Traditional marriage is under assault by those bent on restructuring our culture, and the inevitable result will be to strengthen the state and reduce individual liberty. Strong

---

52 There are many forces arrayed against the health of the family unit. One of the most powerful is tax policy. The income tax and the death tax combine to make it extremely difficult for you to accumulate wealth that would benefit your succeeding generations. In fact, our entire monetary system, with its deliberate inflationary policy, is designed to confiscate your wealth over time. Other anti-family forces include state-controlled education, state supremacy in medical matters, and state control of housing and food.

families create a social safety net; members of large, well-connected families depend on each other for jobs and education, provide financial assistance for each other when medical or economic tragedy strikes, provide advice and moral support when relationships suffer, and teach younger parents how to cope with the challenges of child-rearing.

Naturally, then, any state action that weakens the family will create more vulnerable citizens dependent upon the state for the things a strong family would otherwise provide.

Strong, traditional families have less crime, less poverty, fewer children born out of wedlock, longer life spans, and less depression.[53] It's no wonder, then, that the family is the fundamental unit of society. Where families are strong, the family members benefit. When God formed a nation on this earth, he started with a family; the twelve sons of Jacob. The entire nation of Israel was one large extended family.

Marriage is society's fundamental institution. Those who wish to establish the state as the supreme authority in society have targeted marriage for destruction. The best way to weaken individuals is to attack their support structure–the family. And the best way to attack families is to undermine its foundation–marriage. By undermining marriage, the state destroys the basis of a family, thereby putting all its members at peril. Then it promises to provide all those things a family was better-suited to provide in the first place; social, economic, physical, and emotional security. See how this works?

The first marriage was instituted between three parties; a man, a woman, and God. Marriage stands before God and

53 See, e.g., "New research: How Traditional Families Help Children Succeed," *Liturgical*, July 24, 2009 (http://liturgical.wordpress.com/2009/07/24/new-research-how-traditional-families-help-children-conservative-values-education/).

none other. It is by agreement between individuals, and the state has no place in it. There is no basis in the Bible for making marriage conditional upon state sanction.

It doesn't matter how we alter or redefine it, marriage before God is always and only as He defined it. When King David committed adultery with Bathsheba and then murdered her husband Uriah, God told him that what he had done in secret to Uriah would be done to David in public: "I will take thy wives before thine eyes, and give them unto thy neighbor, and he shall lie with thy wives in the sight of this sun."

But then notice what happens later: "Absalom went in unto his father's concubines in the sight of all Israel." The point is that while we have created a social distinction between wives and concubines, God did not; in his eyes, as between the man and the woman, a concubine is still a wife. Man can redefine marriage all he likes, but it changes nothing in God's eyes.

Remember that the assault on marriage is part of an overarching goal of destroying the family. Strong families create independence and individual autonomy, which are incompatible with statism. We must vigorously defend traditional marriage if we hope to preserve the benefits of a strong family and protect our individual liberties.

There are many socioeconomic and cultural issues tied to the government's involvement in marriage, and extricating ourselves from this situation is going to be difficult. When you have a cancer in your organs, you have to remove it very carefully, or the surgery itself will kill you. The goal eventually is to get the government entirely out of the business of defining and approving marriage, but in the meantime we need to make sure the government doesn't define marriage *badly,* in a way that will destroy families, weaken individuals, and make us all dependent upon the state.

However, a federal amendment defining marriage is not the way to do it. Some have suggested that we need this amendment to stop rogue judges from recognizing homosexual marriages, but the cure would be worse than the illness. To put the power of defining marriage into the hands of a federal government that already has almost total power over our lives would be disastrous. Our problem is that the federal government has too much power – granting it yet more power would be senseless.

This issue illustrates better than any other the absolute incompatibility between statism and liberty. There is no solution involving the state. It has no business injecting itself into the definition of marriage in the first place.

14

STATE CONTROL OF JOBS

Whenever the government intervenes in the relation between employer and employee, it creates distortions of natural free market dynamics. As is always the case, liberty is the sine qua non[54] of prosperity. Government interference with a free market always reduces overall prosperity.

Minimum Wage

Minimum wage laws create unemployment by forcing the employer to pay more than what the employee's services are worth. This makes the employer less competitive, less profitable, and forces him to lay off employees. The unemployed worker now goes on welfare, which requires the government to raise taxes (or print money, which causes prices to rise, which makes everyone's money worth less). This causes the employer to become even less profitable. Some businesses fail, reducing the number of employers, which in turn, reduces the number of jobs available. There is now an oversupply of potential employees, making their services even less valuable, creating even less demand for their services, and the cycle continues.

---

54 *Sine qua non* is Latin for "without which nothing." It identifies something that is indispensable for the existence of something else.

Meanwhile, as inflation rises, the rich become richer because money is never injected evenly into the economy – it goes to the richest people first. These people have the "first take" at the increased supply of money, before prices rise, and they acquire assets at bargain prices. By the time the increased supply of money trickles down to lower-income people, the total amount of money in the economy has been devalued, and they have become poorer.

A free market causes the rich to become richer, but it also causes everyone in the system to become richer as well by increasing prosperity in the entire economic system.

The solution is not to have wage controls, but to eliminate them and remove other impediments to business profitability.

Child Labor Laws

Protecting children from bad working conditions and unscrupulous employers is a morally laudable goal, but government-created child labor laws have hidden consequences that are even worse.

First, child labor laws make children unemployable, which eliminates their opportunities to become skilled and productive. They have nearly eliminated the mentor-apprentice system of learning. A century ago, a typical 18-year-old was already a skilled tradesman or professional with 6 or 8 years of experience, well able to provide a living for himself or his family.

Look at 18-year-olds today. Most are unskilled, poorly educated by the government schools, and unemployable except in low-wage positions, which are hard to find because minimum wage laws have caused very low demand for their services. Their best prospect is to extend their unproductive adolescence into their twenties by going to government-funded universities where they will continue their mediocre education and land in a highly competitive job market, already heavily burdened with debt.

They will have less opportunity to accumulate wealth for their own families, and their children will have even less opportunity than they did.

The second dismal consequence of child labor laws is that they reduce the ability of children to escape abusive conditions at home. If your father was a worthless drunk, in a free market you could go find a job even at the age of 10 or 12. You could then slip some money to your mother and siblings, or bring groceries home. As it is, no employer will hire you because it's illegal, even if you found an employer who would pay you well and provide a favorable working environment.

Because a few children were employed by a few unscrupulous employers, the state has forbidden all children to be employed, even those who want to work for good employers who want to hire them.

A third unfortunate result is that child labor laws cause a decline in birth rates by subsidizing childlessness. These laws are a wealth transfer from families with many children to families with none. They deprive the large family of income they would otherwise have earned; meanwhile, wages rise because of labor shortages, and these higher wages go to adults. The economic value of children declines, and the birth rate decreases.

The solution is to eliminate government interference in the job markets. There will always be a few bad employers, but in a free market they don't last long. Other employers will compete for the workers, enticing them with better pay and/or better working conditions.

15

UNIONS

In a free market, unions are a perfectly fine idea. Workers join a union and bargain collectively with employers to obtain desired pay and working conditions. Other unions compete for membership by offering better results and charging lower membership fees. Employers are free to refuse a union contract, but good unions make their proposals palatable to employers and union members alike. Unions that make unreasonable demands fail to reach agreement with the employer, and members leave that union to join one that gets results.

In a free market, employees who don't want to join a union are free to negotiate their own agreements. Those who want to leave negotiations to the experts join a union.

Of course, none of this bears any resemblance to the way unions really work, because the government gives unions special privileges. In reality, you don't have two parties (the employer and the union) bargaining on a level playing field. Instead, the government takes sides in the negotiations between unions and employers. Politicians grant the unions special privileges in exchange for their votes. Instead of putting the employer and union on equal footing in the negotiations, the unions get a government-mandated upper hand.

In exchange, the unions contribute primarily to Democrat candidates, since they're the most reliable Marxists.

With government sanction, the unions can "picket," which is a kind of legalized riot. It's why we have "union thugs."

As a result, employers have to pay the union members more than the true market value of their services. The employer becomes less profitable; its stock value drops and its shareholders lose money. Some employees get better pay, but others lose their jobs. Once again, government interference in the market results in unemployment and an overall reduction of productivity and wealth in the economy.

It's worth noting that the federal government has no constitutional authority in the first place to give unions special privileges in contract negotiations. The National Labor Relations Act must be repealed in its entirety, and the National Labor Relations Board dismantled.

—— ∞∞∞ ——

There is an important difference between private sector unions and government employee unions.

Private unions negotiate against a private-sector employer on behalf of the employees. The employer is often portrayed as a big, fat, cigar-chomping, jet-flying evil tycoon, and the union comes to the rescue of the downtrodden, slave-wage-earning overworked employees.

Government unions represent employees who often earn twice as much as their private-sector counterparts, and the employer is the taxpayer who earns half as much as his employee. The government union represents an employee who is already receiving a direct wealth-transfer from the taxpayer, and the question is only "how much more can we take from taxpayers?"

All unions collect membership dues from the employees they represent. The union leaders collect huge salaries, and then spend millions on campaign contributions for Democrats, because the Democratic party is the one that supports the Marxist principles that benefit the unions.

But public sector unions are a special case – they're a kind of branch of government, and their dues and activities are all tax-supported. Government employees are paid out of tax dollars, and the unions collect membership dues from them, so taxpayers are funding Democratic Party campaigns.

This is why there was such hysteria when the State of Wisconsin passed a law reducing the power of public sector unions.[55] Democrats and union leaders sent protesters from all around the country to invade and damage the Wisconsin State Capitol, issue death threats, and intimidate legislators and citizens. Wisconsin's public school teachers earned an average salary and benefits package worth over $100,000 annually, but when asked to pay just 6% of the cost of their health insurance, they rioted.

No one in his right mind would behave that way unless incited by people with ulterior motives. The rent-a-mobs at the state capitol were union thugs from other states doing the bidding of national union leaders interested in nothing more than protecting their gravy train. They had their place at the public trough like the rest of the government. It was just about the money and the power.

So when government unions negotiate higher salaries and benefits for the government employees they represent, you, the taxpayer, are the evil fat-cat employer they oppose. You're the enemy. Those rioters at the Wisconsin State

---

55 Scott Walker, "Why I'm Fighting In Wisconsin," *The Wall Street Journal*, Mar. 10, 2011 (http://online.wsj.com/article/SB10001424052748704132204576190260787805984.html).

Capitol were foaming at the mouth because of their hatred for you, who wanted to force them to pay 6% of the cost of their health insurance.

16

THE UNIQUE AMERICAN PHILOSOPHY

"I would rather be exposed to the inconveniences attending too much liberty than to those attending too small a degree of it."

– Thomas Jefferson

The Founders of the United States had a view of themselves and their nation that was unique in the world. They believed that the blessings of liberty were far more precious than any privilege or benefit that could be obtained from kings, governors, presidents, or other rulers in government. To them, the only legitimate function of government was to protect life, liberty, and the pursuit of happiness, and they established a government that was authorized to do that and little else.

Certainly the concept of liberty was not perfectly put into practice at the founding, but it was done to a greater extent than almost anywhere else in the world. Private property ownership, free enterprise, capitalism, and extremely limited government in general liberated an entire nation of individuals and allowed their ingenuity to flourish. After the abolition of slavery, there were no ruling classes as there were in other countries; individuals from rich to poor had the same economic opportunities, and the United States became the most prosperous nation in history.

Things are very different today. Can you think of a single aspect of your conduct that isn't regulated by the government? From the clothes you wear to the house you live in, the food you eat, the car you drive, and even the air you breathe, everything you do and everywhere you go, the government is there dictating the conditions of your existence. The founders wouldn't recognize this country; it's not at all what they created.

As of this writing, the government is preparing to choke off the last frontier of liberty left in the world; the FCC has announced plans to regulate news and information delivery on the Internet. The news organizations, usually diehard defenders of the First Amendment, have no objection because the Internet is their only direct competition. They are happy to let the government seize power over speech, so long as it profits them.

They're being short-sighted, though. Until now, the government has had no need to stifle the mainstream media, because they're all on the same team. For the last two or three decades, the newspapers and TV news have been little more than the propaganda department of Big State. But once the government has set a precedent for regulating the news, that power will only expand. For now, the government and the news company executives agree about how to deliver state-approved "information" to the public. One day they will disagree, and the state will dictate how it's to be done.

The American philosophy of government used to be unique in the world; it used to be the only country on Earth whose citizens had no rulers, but now it is like all the rest. Why would Americans extinguish the last beacon of liberty on the planet?

To answer this question, we need to identify two different groups of people; the politicians, and the citizens. It's no mystery that politicians want more and more power and are never satisfied. We all get this; we don't approve, but we get it. The real puzzle is why formerly free American citizens have given up their liberty. There are still a few freedom-loving people, and they're baffled because they can't fathom why people would willingly allow politicians to take away their liberties and rule over them.

There are two answers. On one hand is the personal motivation of the voters; it's their greed, envy, and laziness. By definition, most people are not the richest people among us. This is self-evident: Only 2% of the people are in the 98th percentile in terms of wealth. That leaves 98 out of 100 people who can get greedy and envious of the wealth of those top two percent. When the government offers them the opportunity to steal the rich people's money and redistribute it to others, greedy, envious people jump at the chance. After all, the rich have so much money, they don't need it, right? They ignore the fact that stealing is reprehensible and morally depraved, and just because a large majority of people agree to it doesn't change that fact.

Corrupt, power-hungry politicians have made a sinister agreement with greedy, envious citizens. "You give us the power," the politician says, "and we'll soak the rich and give you the money." The citizens are only too happy to agree, and that's how we've lost our liberties. Now the politicians rule over us, and most of the citizens allow it because at least they're sticking it to the rich.

There will always be those who covet the property of others. In a free society, most of those people suppress their feelings and even feel ashamed of them and reform their own hearts. Those who succumb to their desire to take someone else's property are treated as criminals; they are punished and forced to restore the victim.

In a welfare state like ours, however, there is no stigma attached to greed or covetousness. In fact, it is institutionalized, made an integral part of the function of government, and the assault against private property is given an air or label of legitimacy.

That's why the have-nots elect socialists and have them take from the haves. It starts with petty jealousy, plain old fashioned coveting what someone richer has, and it ends with legalized theft.

And this brings us to the second reason why Americans have given up their liberties. In a very real sense, we had no choice. It was inevitable, and a necessary consequence of our form of government. In fact, it is the very nature of all governments. We'll explore this in the next chapter, but the summary is this: a government is an association of people who maintain a monopoly of violence in order to exploit the people in its territory, primarily by taking their money against their will, under the threat of violence.

That is, a government institutionalizes theft. You can't expect a government to defend liberty when its very existence depends on the continued, systematic violation of your liberties.

17

THE AMERICAN FORM OF GOVERNMENT

The founders of the United States debated what kind of government to establish when they broke away from England. They had two serious contenders; a monarchy or a democracy.[56]

Monarchies are inherently and quite openly a class-oriented form of government.[57] There is a ruling class – the royal family – which owns the government and has a monopoly on taxation. The subjects of the king have no right to determine the laws of the nation or its actions in relation to other nations. The king alone has this right, although we'll see later how that right is practically limited by the consent of the subjects.

Democracies are also a class-oriented form of government, but class-consciousness is suppressed and covered up by the pretense of popular representation. Because anyone theoretically can become one of the ruling government

---

56 The US was established as a republic, but it has always had a democratic electoral process. As suffrage has been expanded over the last two centuries, the republican structure has been weakened and the democratic characteristics have worsened.

57 On the characteristics of monarchies and democracies, read the excellent book by Hoppe, *Democracy: The God that Failed.*

officials, there is an illusion of classlessness. But the truth is that democracies exhibit a constant struggle between various classes and classifications of people who are attempting to obtain a ruling majority. There is always a group in power cramming their rules down everyone else's throat, and the struggle is always over who will dominate.

Democracies are systemically more wasteful and socially destructive than monarchies. I say "systemically" because the destructiveness is built into the system. Individual kings might be worse, and individual democratic administrations might be better at one time or another, but this relates to the character and moral strength of those in office, whereas I'm talking about the inherent characteristics of the governmental system; the inescapable, irresistible incentives that determine how people behave over the long term.

In a democracy – or a democratic republic, or any other system that uses a democratic process to form the government – the rulers don't actually own the public property of the government. Since they don't own it, they can't profit from its capital value, so they don't care about it; they become wasteful and reckless with the resources of the nation.

In a democracy, if a government official doesn't spend right now, he won't be able to spend later. Because a king owns the resources – the land, the money, and all the productivity of the nation – he knows he can benefit from the future value of his holdings. A president does not now, and will not in the future, own the public property of the United States. If he doesn't tax now, he won't benefit from the future wealth of the nation created by low tax rates. At least a king has an incentive to keep taxes low.

A king also has a powerful incentive to maintain his country's economic health and stability. He cannot for long devalue his own currency without eventually cutting his own throat. A president, on the other hand, doesn't give a hoot about the future value of the currency,[58] but only about what he can do with it now. The one who gives away the most stuff is the one who gets elected. A king doesn't have such competition, and he doesn't want to devalue his own holdings.

Sure, some kings are morally deficient and short-sighted, and do stupid things. And true, some individuals in a democratic government have a stronger sense of responsibility than others and may, by pure force of character, overcome some of the temptation to be wasteful, but the tendency to waste is built into the democratic governmental system. It is relentless and powerful. Most people can't resist the tendency to spend right now.

In a monarchy, the king has a built-in incentive that appeals to his own self-interest – the better his stewardship of his kingdom, the richer he'll be. This is a systemic limitation on his incentive to exercise too much power over his subjects.

Another check on his power is the class-consciousness itself. If you're not part of the royal family, you're a subject of the king, and you're acutely aware of your lower status. You're already somewhat annoyed about it, so you're very sensitive to what you perceive to be unfair behavior by the king. In a democracy, you don't tend to have such a high sensitivity to unfairness, and so you tolerate very high tax rates, intense regulation of public and private life, and outrageous behavior by public officials. In fact, because of

---

58 Again, I'm talking about the character of the system – some individual elected officials do in fact care about the value of the currency, but they eventually lose to opponents who get elected by promising to give away more stuff. It's harder to raise taxes than it is to devalue (inflate) the currency, so politicians always inflate as much as they can. This makes more money available for them to spend right now, even though it will be worth a little less tomorrow.

your reduced sensitivity to unfairness, you and everyone else tend to act in ways that are unfair toward others.

Monarchies historically have much lower tax rates than democracies. They tend to expand their borders by acquisition rather than conquest. They tend to have a smaller number of ruling government officials. They tend to have greater financial privacy, less regulation of business and property, more stable economies, fewer socio-economic classifications, higher standards of living, and more equal distributions of private wealth within the non-ruling class.

The attractive thing about a democracy over a monarchy is that everyone has a say in their government – it allows everyone a chance, at least in theory, to be a part of the ruling class. All you have to do is secure a voting majority and bingo, you have the power to dominate others. You will then take money and liberty from those who used to be your fellow citizens. Isn't it wonderful?

—— ∞∞ ——

When you give someone a lot of power, you can't count on his character to use it well – it's a feature of human nature that power corrupts. You have to have systemic checks on his power, and the best kind of check of all is a limitation of the power itself.

The King of England had left the founders of the United States with a particularly bad taste in their mouths for monarchs, but they were without exception opposed to democracy. The debates were contentious.

In the end, they established a republican aristocracy in which our elected representatives governed within a constitutionally limited range of powers – eighteen enumerated powers, to be precise.

It seemed like a decent enough idea. Everyone – at least those who enjoyed suffrage[59] – would have some input in their governance, but power would be limited so that government could not get out of control and destroy civilization with high taxes and regulation. So they created a federal government that could only do a few specific things.

Unfortunately, the founders underestimated man's thirst for power, and the government has devolved into the democracy we see today. Bit by bit they amended the Constitution to pave the way for democratic processes (like the extensions of suffrage and the Seventeenth Amendment, which provided for the popular election of senators, instead of their appointment by the state legislatures).

From my research, I don't think it occurred to them that politicians would eventually just ignore their constitutional limitations and exercise forbidden powers,[60] and I'm almost certain that they would be flabbergasted to see how we citizens tolerate their illegitimate rule. Those guys were fresh out of a bloody revolution in which they risked it all to secure liberty, and now we have squandered it. They were made of entirely different stuff than the American politicians of today.

What we have now, therefore, is a democratic republic with no de facto constitutional limitations, checked only by the population's limit of tolerance for perceived illegitimacy. Let's see the results. In discussing the rise of the democratic republics since 1913, Hoppe observes as follows:

> *Compulsory military service has become almost universal, foreign and civil wars have increased in*

---

59 Suffrage: the right to vote.

60 The anti-federalists vigorously argued against the enumerated powers themselves, considering them alone to be too broad, (see, e.g., Anti-Federalist Paper No. 17), but I'm not aware of any of them arguing that the federal government would frankly ignore its Constitutional limitations.

*frequency and in brutality.... Internally, democratic
republicanism has led to permanently rising taxes, debts,
and public employment. It has led to the destruction of
the gold standard, unparalleled paper-money inflation,
and increased protectionism and migration controls.
Even the most fundamental private law provisions have
been perverted by an unabating flood of legislation and
regulation.... [T]he institutions of marriage and family
have been increasingly weakened, the number of children
has declined, and the rates of divorce, illegitimacy, single
parenthood, singledom, and abortion have increased....
And the rates of crime, structural unemployment, welfare
dependency, parasitism, negligence, recklessness,
incivility, psychopathy, and hedonism have increased.*[61]

These are all results of the systemic characteristics of
democracy. When you can just take someone else's property
and call it your own without earning it, it brings on a cascade
of bad character traits, which are then manifested in society
at large. It's just common sense; wealth transfers like welfare
programs, social security, and price controls are simply
legalized theft, so it shouldn't surprise you when the whole
country starts acting like a bunch of scoundrels.

We're witnessing the decline of western civilization.
The basis of a civilized society is recognition and protection
of private property rights; all forms of welfare are
institutionalized crime, which is inherently antithetical to
civilized society. You can reverse this, if you really want to,
but you'll have to stop tolerating the cause of the problem,
which is the fact that the government operates a welfare state.

---

61 Hoppe, *Democracy: The God that Failed*, 42.

18

TAXES

Taxation – a monopoly right to take money from people by the threat of force – is the core characteristic of any state. No other institution can legally tax. The Mafia might extort money in a protection racket, and it's illegal. The government does exactly the same thing, but it's legal.

When you take something from someone against his will, it's theft. If I go to your house and hold you at gunpoint to take your money, it is theft. If the government demands your money under threat of arrest and imprisonment, they call it taxation, but it's still theft. The entire business of taxation is, at the bottom line, a criminal enterprise.

One way governments excuse this is by arguing that what they're providing in exchange is "necessary." Let's concede just for a moment that that's true. Let's suppose that, in fact, there would be no public roads unless the government taxed us to build them. The fact remains that the tax is theft, and the mere desire to have public roads does not justify it.

You might argue that you want and need public roads, and are happy to pay the taxes. Fine, but all that means is that the government is taking *your* money by consent, not mine, for I still object. The fact that you want a road doesn't justify anyone stealing my money so you can have one. Even if a world without publicly-funded roads would be significantly different, it still doesn't make theft acceptable; we don't excuse theft because of popular demand for the stolen good. But let's step back a moment and examine the claim that only the government can provide roads. How did we get started with this weird idea? The historical fact is that there have always been private roads, even today in the United States. Are we to believe that brilliant American entrepreneurs are the first in history to forget how to build a "road network" business? For that matter, you could ask the same about literally anything the government provides or produces.

Another way in which the concept of taxation has gotten twisted is in the attempt to come up with a system of "fair" taxes. There's no way to determine a "fair share" of taxes, because taxing is unfair in the first place. Talking about how to "fairly" distribute tax burdens is like a gang of thieves in a bank asking each other "what's the fairest way to rob these good citizens?"

The government is just an association of people, like a partnership or corporation, which has assigned itself certain unique privileges. But what sets them apart from everyone else is that these people take for themselves a monopoly of aggression and compulsion in the form of taking money from people under threat of force.

There's a flip-side of taxation; another activity only the state is allowed to do – counterfeiting. When the government steals from you by inflating the money supply, which causes a devaluation of the currency, it is called "fiscal policy." But when you do exactly the same thing, it is called "counterfeiting," and you'll go to prison.

The case of Bernard Von NotHaus is instructive.[62] He was the creator of the Liberty Dollar, a coin he circulated

---

62 "Fake gold and silver Ron Paul coins seized," MSNBC.com, Nov. 16, 2007 (http://www.msnbc.msn.com/id/21836699/ns/politics-decision_08/); Federal Bureau of Investigation, *Defendant Convicted of Minting His Own Currency*, http://charlotte.fbi.gov/dojpressrel/pressrel11/ce031811.htm (March 11, 2011).

as currency. He was convicted, among other things, of making currency, sentenced to a prison term, fined, and his goods were confiscated by the government. In announcing the verdict, the prosecutor said, "attempts to undermine the legitimate currency of this country are simply a unique form of domestic terrorism." This is darkly ironic because circulating competing currency actually would have the opposite effect; it would improve the value of the dollar. When a better money comes along, in order to compete the dollar must improve its value. It is government fiscal policy (reserve banking, inflation, and debt) that undermines the currency, not competition.

What this illustrates is that the government is not interested in improving the value of the dollar, but in protecting its currency monopoly. The government protects its monopoly of currency so that it may continue to inflate, because inflation is just the flip-side of taxation; when you can't tax more because it isn't politically expedient, you just inflate the money supply by printing money.

Taxation is simply how the state sustains itself, and it provides services so it can convince us to pay the tax. The more it can convince us we need it, the more it can tax us without facing revolution. There are many tools at the state's disposal to do the convincing. Let's examine a few.

State Controlled Schools. The purpose of public schools is not to provide an education, but to mold children into a state-support network. They teach the children not that they are free individuals in the world, but that they are "members of society," with obligations to society, as if society were an entity or personality who could demand rights and respect. The truth is that there is no such thing as society in and of itself; it can't be owed anything, it can't buy or sell anything and it can't be offended or harmed in any way.

When they say "society," they really mean "state." The schools teach children to be *good statists.*

Public schools are the ideal forum for increasing the size of government, because any attempt to reduce education budgets is so easily demagogued as an attack on helpless children. If you voice any opposition to the waste, fraud, and poor performance of teachers, you'll be called a threat to the welfare of children. So education budgets always swell, the quality of education always falls, the schools hire more workers, build more buildings, buy more buses, serve more free meals, and the children are used as pawns so government school employees can go on parasitizing the taxpayer.

State Controlled Media. When the state controls and regulates corporations and dispenses favors at will, there can be no independent media, for all the newspapers, television networks, and radio stations are owned by corporations which depend on the state for their continued existence. This explains why virtually all media outlets are statist. Newspapers, radio, and TV serve as the state mouthpiece, a daily propaganda machine whose primary function is to advocate for the continuous growth and expansion of government. Rarely do you ever hear media outlets calling for lower taxes, fewer services, or reduced regulations. Whatever the problem, the solution is always more government.

Worse, in the case of radio and television, the state owns the airwaves and licenses them. During the early 1900s radio stations were "homesteading" the airwaves, but the government was worried about having no control over this particularly influential form of mass communication. Even as the courts were developing a solid body of property rights laws to sort out the private market for radio waves, the government asserted the pretext of "chaos" and seized the airwaves. Now you can't broadcast your message – political or otherwise – without government permission.

The natural tendency is for the media to become less and less objective over time. Media Malpractice[63] is a fascinating documentary that chronicles the open media bias in favor of Barack Obama during his first presidential campaign. News anchors and reporters who in previous years were cagey and sly about their biases now openly admitted their bias on the air.

National Public Radio and the Public Broadcasting Service are directly funded by the government, so their state bias is inherent.

State Controlled Crises. The state can manufacture all sorts of crises in order to increase demand for the services it provides, and thereby create an excuse to raise taxes to meet the increased demand. Government agents are quite explicit about the fact that crises provide them an opportunity to expand government in ways they couldn't otherwise do. White House Chief of Staff Rahm Emmanuel is famous for saying in 2008 that "you never want a serious crisis to go to waste. And what I mean by that, it's an opportunity to do things you think you could not do before."[64]

He was talking about taking advantage of a crisis that just happened along (the Fannie Mae mortgage crisis), but the state can create crises in many ways. Manipulating the currency to create inflation causes economic hardship and greater dependency on welfare; banning oil recovery causes fuel shortages, increasing the price of fuel and virtually everything else, and people demand tighter regulation of price-gouging oil companies; forcing banks to make bad loans

---

63 Media Malpractice, official web site (http://www.howobamagotelected.com/).

64 Wall Street Journal Digital Network, "Rahm Emanuel on the Opportunities of Crisis," http://www.youtube.com/watch?v=_mzcbXi1Tkk.

causes them (and other industries) to fail, which necessitates federal "bailouts" in which the government becomes part owner of the banks, car companies, and insurers.

Maybe the mortgage crisis didn't just "happen along" after all. As in Panama in the late 1980s, the government can deliberately provoke incidents which then "require" military intervention, at enormous expense to taxpayers and enormous profit to the military-industrial complex. In all these cases, the state directly or indirectly causes the crisis it swoops down to solve. In every case the government gets bigger.

State Controlled Intellectual Class. The state's power grows only as large as public opinion will let it, and public opinion has always been managed by the intellectual class of a nation. Today these are the media commentators, scientists, and university professors. All of these levers of public opinion are in state control.

State control of the media has already been discussed.

State control of scientists and university professors is simply a matter of tax-funded educational and research grants. A great number of scientists and professors depend on the state to fund research into any number of social and scientific issues: global warming, evolution, welfare programs, gun control, pollution, economics, education, and so on. The research produced by state-controlled researchers and then reported by state-controlled reporters nearly always supports a statist position on any given issue.

The government funds the research. If you want more funding, your research results had better support the government.

19

THE CRIMINALIZATION OF SELF-DEFENSE

Whenever I enter a "gun-free zone" such as a university campus, I am painfully aware that if a criminal goes on a murderous rampage, he's not going to care about the prohibition against guns on campus. But if I take a gun on campus to defend myself, I'm automatically a criminal. If someone discovers my gun, I can lose my handgun carry permit forever, and if I'm charged with a felony I'll lose the right to own any guns, even at home.

This sort of insanity is the norm for gun control advocates. There's no sensible reason to ban guns on campus – it's already a crime to murder someone. All the gun-banners have done is to make good citizens unable to defend themselves. They don't say it this way, of course – after all, you're still free to defend yourself with your book bag or your bare hands. But by forbidding me to carry a gun on campus, I have effectively been deprived of the best means of defending myself. I mean, the criminal brought a gun to do his killing, not a book bag.

The consequence is that self-defense has effectively been criminalized.

It's almost impossible to understand why anyone would advocate such a stupid law. But there is an explanation. The purpose in creating gun-free zones is not to reduce the risk of gun deaths in those areas. Rather, it's an incremental step in accomplishing an altogether different goal; disarming citizens.

Consider the ridiculous idea that we need a Transportation Security Administration to assure security on airplanes. The government takes a completely nonsensical approach to the very concept of security. Left to their own decisions, humans assess the risk analysis of traveling completely differently than the government does. When you fly, by far the riskiest part of your trip is to and from the airport. How much liberty would you willingly sacrifice in order to make highway travel safer? Would you give up private transportation and leave it to the government to shuttle you around everywhere you go?

We'd be better off if the airlines were in charge of airplane security. They have a built-in incentive to provide whatever level of security their customers desire. In a free world, airline companies would compete for the best balance of security and convenience. Different airlines would have different procedures, and travelers would choose the one they prefer. The informed traveler interested in greater security would choose more intrusive security procedures, and the one more interested in convenience would fly with a company that had more streamlined procedures.

A smart airline company would develop a way to provide a high level of security with greater convenience, with procedures acceptable to its potential customers. Competition would cause the airlines to tune their procedures for whatever balance of security and convenience travelers demand. For travelers who wanted extreme security, an airline would provide the desired level of security. For those who wanted total convenience, airlines would have them sign a personal security waiver and pass them through without so much as a bag check.

For travelers who wanted to provide their own security, an airline would provide "armed traveler" flights and require ammunition that would stop a would-be hijacker without taking down the plane. Considering the proven drop in violent crime in states that allow citizens to carry concealed weapons, we have all the evidence we need to conclude that safety would be greatly enhanced, and all while providing an alternative for travelers who refuse to fly with armed citizens.

That's liberty, and as always, it provides better results than the government's coercion can ever do.

And that's precisely the point. An armed citizenry has fewer threats to its security, and less need for the government. If the *citizens* have the same weapons as the lunatics in the government, they can't be dominated. And if you can't dominate people, what's the point of being in the government?

20

THE POLICE STATE MENTALITY

Joe, Sarah, and their two boys drove to a local grocery store one day in November. They just had to get a few items, so they left the children in the minivan watching a movie. When they returned, there were three police cars with their lights flashing, and when Joe and Sarah realized their van was surrounded, they thought something horrible had happened. They rushed to the van. One of the officers was talking through the open window to Josh, the twelve-year-old, and another was poking around in the van. Ben, the three-year-old, was watching the movie and snacking on some sliced apples.

"What's going on?" Joe asked the third officer.

"Are these your children?" the officer demanded.

"Yes, are they hurt?" Joe started toward the van.

"Stay where you are, sir."

Joe probably heard the words, but in his concern it didn't process, and he continued to the van.

"Sir! Stay here! I need to ask you some questions!" While the officer focused on Joe, Sarah made her way to the van and checked on the children.

Joe glanced at her, then turned to the officer. "What is it?"

"It's against the law to leave young children unattended in the car."

Joe blinked. "The little guy? He's not unattended; we left Josh with him."

Sarah quickly appraised the situation. While Joe was busy with the officer, she opened the rear hatch and began loading the groceries in the back.

The officer didn't respond directly. "We received a complaint that your children were left unattended in the car. We're just making sure they're safe."

"Looks like they're fine to me." Joe said. "If it gets too cold, Josh knows how to crank the engine and turn on the heater." He almost said that Josh knew how to *drive* the van, but thought better of it.

"I understand," the officer said, "but it's against the law to leave children unattended in the car."

"I know. I'm saying I didn't. Josh is here to take care of him."

"How old is the older one again?" the officer asked.

"Twelve. How old does he have to be?"

The officer didn't actually know, so he skirted the issue. "We're just checking into a complaint, sir. I needed to ask you some questions. We had to check into it."

"With three cruisers and all your lights flashing?"

Sarah had the car loaded and had jumped into the driver's seat. The van was running.

"Why are you searching the car?" Joe asked.

"Sir, we're just looking into the complaint."

"Are we under arrest?" Joe asked.

The officer looked around at the others and hesitated a moment.

"No, sir. You're free to go."

With a little investigation, Joe and Sarah learned that a passerby had seen the children in the van and complained to a security guard. His response was to call the police, and this led to the incident when Joe and Sarah returned to the van. They asked the security guard why he called the police instead of just looking into it himself, because if he had, he would have seen that the children were just fine.

His stunning reply was that he had no choice, but this was clearly not true; there was no law and not even a store policy requiring him to call the police. But he had been conditioned into a police state mentality that said "I cannot exercise the normal common sense of a self-aware human being. I must get the State involved, no matter how intrusive it might be."

At the end of this chapter we'll look into how this incident could have been avoided in a country that had not devolved into a police state.

<hr />

You've probably heard the term "sheeple." It describes a lot of things that are wrong with people. Human beings should not be treated like herd animals, but it's even worse when they consent to it. That's what "sheeple" are; people who allow themselves to be treated like dumb animals.

This is the mindset of people who are conditioned into a police state mentality. It's the idea that the most important characteristic of good citizenship is submission to state authority. This is what some people mean when they say "I'm a law-abiding citizen."

I'm not advocating that we become non-law-abiding citizens. I'm saying that what makes us good citizens is an entirely different thing; that our true worth as a citizen is not determined by reference to the laws of our nation.

The people who founded this country thought this way. They measured their value as a citizen without reference to the state. In their way of thinking, a good citizen provided for himself and those in his care, was hardworking, productive, charitable, considerate of others, responsible with his material blessings, generous, respectful, honest, hospitable... in other words, good citizenship depended on good character. His worth as a citizen was judged without reference to the wishes of rulers, governors, kings, a President, or a legislature.

To the extent a good citizen considered the laws at all, it was a very different kind of laws than we have today. Whereas the laws today control every aspect of your life and behavior, in those days it was understood that the purpose of government was simply to protect the liberty of all individuals. Yes, I understand that not all individuals had liberty, for we did have slavery at the founding of the nation and for many years later. The ideals in the Constitution had not yet been perfectly applied to all individuals. But the solution is to make liberty available to everyone, not make all citizens slaves of the state.

Anyway, just abiding by the law does not by itself make you a good citizen. The people of this nation were good citizens long before they had the thousands of pages of laws that ruled their lives.

Let me give you an example. When I was a child, we were expected to "always be prepared." It was perfectly good citizenship to take a pocketknife to school, into a courtroom, or even on an airplane. Try that today. I'm an even better citizen today than I was as a child; I'm more productive, hospitable, responsible, and so on. If anything, my character has improved, and so if you judged the quality of my citizenship by my character, you'd say I was a better citizen today than I was years ago. Yet, if I took a pocketknife into a courtroom I'd be treated like a criminal. My worth as a citizen is judged not by reference to my character, but by reference to the state. We no longer judge a citizen's worth by the quality of his character, but by how well he submits to the state.

That's a police state mentality.

The police state mentality is in every way at odds with good character. Government welfare takes the place of virtues like hard work, honesty, and productivity. Parents accept free school lunches instead of providing the most basic needs for their children, like food. In fact, just by giving the state primary responsibility for their children's education, they abdicate one of the fundamental responsibilities of parenting.

In a police state, citizens become helpless in the face of emergencies, because they have become used to the idea of having someone else take care of them. They are conditioned to trust their government, unlike the founders of our nation, who distrusted government. In the minds of Americans today, the government is the source of their security and safety. Just look at the names of all these agencies: Social *Security*, Homeland *Security*, the Occupational *Safety* and Health Administration, the Product *Safety* Commission, the National Highway Traffic *Safety* Administration, the Transportation *Security* Administration, the Environmental *Protection* Agency... the list goes on. Since they believe the government will provide for their security, they don't prepare to take of themselves, and when disaster strikes they are helpless.

This conditioned dependency on government discourages the virtues of self-reliance, preparedness, common sense, and wisdom. I was watching a Superbowl game one night when we heard a knock at the door. It was a teenage girl who had blown a tire in a pothole. She was driving alone in the country at night and had no idea how to change her tire. Now, I'm not complaining about helping a damsel in distress – actually, I'm glad to do it, even though I did miss a touchdown. But this girl had no idea what was in her trunk. She had a compact spare tire, but it was flat, and she had no compressor to fill it. What if she hadn't had her flat just a hundred yards from someone's house? It was below freezing and she had only a light jacket and no flashlight.

Many people are not prepared to handle even the most common mishaps in life. So when a serious natural disaster strikes, these people are not merely inconvenienced by their lack of self-reliance; often they are frankly in mortal danger.

The police state mentality is, of course, manifested in the behavior of some of the state's police officers; they show less courtesy, respect, and common sense toward civilians, whom they consider to be lower-class citizens. They have an authoritarian attitude. Thuggery, bullying, and the use of excessive force become commonplace.

I once parked in the street to eat at a local pizza restaurant. Suddenly, my son told me the car was being towed. Outside, the officer told me I was illegally parked, but there were no signs forbidding it. He said it was illegal anyway. I offered to move the car, but he told me I would have to pay the tow bill since the truck had already arrived, and he gave me a ticket for "parking on a hill." I sent a check to pay the parking ticket, but it was returned by a clerk with a note saying that "parking on a hill" did not violate any city ordinance.

So I went to the police station to claim reimbursement for the tow bill. They called the officer to explain the situation, and his justification was that he thought it was unsafe, and he didn't care if there was no ordinance forbidding it, he would have the car towed anyway.

Understand what is going on here. This officer does not consider himself bound by the law. He has a badge, and in his mind that's enough authority for him to determine when to tow a car. The fact that I was legally parked wasn't relevant to him; the only thing that mattered was whether he liked where I parked or not. This is the classic mindset of a tyrant in a police state.

After hurricane Katrina, the local officials displayed an extreme case of police state authoritarianism. They forced people from their homes regardless of whether they had been flooded or otherwise damaged. In some cases, they beat those who refused to leave. They confiscated their guns, depriving them of the ability to defend themselves from marauding gangs. There are many videos on YouTube depicting these gestapo-style tactics.[65]

To their credit, some members of the national guard refused to violate their oaths to uphold the Constitution. One of these is Staff Sergeant Joshua May, whose interview was posted on YouTube by the people at Restore the Republic.[66]

When you watch this video, understand that the reason there is still hope for liberty in America is that there are people willing to resist. Joshua May made it clear that he would not comply with orders to disarm citizens. The people

---

65 See, e.g., NRA Videos, "NRA: The Untold Story of Gun Confiscation After Katrina," http://www.youtube.com/watch?v=-taU9d26wT4&feature=related (March 7, 2007).

66 Lone Lantern, "Staff Sergeant Refuses Gun Grab - Reality Report Special Interview," http://www.youtube.com/watch?v=uLaKsbM0x3g (May 19, 2010).

who will save our country are the ones who will take action to restore our lost liberties, and not merely complain about it. Are you one of them?

Many Americans have been conditioned for life in a police state. One way the government does this training is by offering a bad option and a worse one. As I write this, airline travelers in the US are being conditioned to accept the presence of machines that use dangerous radiation to see through your clothing and display an image of your naked body. We're all used to the metal detectors, but someone invented these "full-body scanners" and got a government contract to install them in airports all over the country.

To condition travelers to get used to them, they get a good-cop bad-cop routine. If they set off the metal detector or are otherwise selected for greater scrutiny, they are offered the choice of a full-body scanner or, if they refuse, they must submit to an "enhanced pat-down." This is a bureaucratic term for sexual assault; the enhanced pat-down involves touching the breasts and genitals.

But it's not really a choice. The government's policy is that once you enter the line at the security checkpoint, you can't back out. So let's suppose you don't like the scanners or the possibility of being fondled by a Transportation Security Officer, but your mother is in the hospital in another state and you urgently need to travel, so you take your chances and hope you don't get selected. No such luck: they pick you, and you refuse the scanner, so they require you to submit to groping. "Never mind," you say. "I'll drive." The government's response? You'll face a $10,000 fine.

There has been quite a public uprising over this issue, but the government is doubling down, even threatening to apply the same procedures to boat, train, and metro travel.[67] It's clear that these procedures have nothing to do with a terrorist threat. All of the terrorist acts that are used as an excuse for these security procedures were committed by men of middle-eastern descent, but the people being searched are men, women, and children of all ages and description, and to date, these procedures have not captured a single terrorist.

The uselessness and stupidity of these procedures is so obvious to the liberty-oriented mind that it's almost impossible to understand why American citizens go along with them. If a department store had such a policy, no one would tolerate it, but somehow when the government does it, people figure it must be necessary, and that's really the only way to explain the insanity of consenting to it. They've been conditioned to let the government do things to them that they would never allow anyone else to do. They're "sheeple." If recent history is any indication, the furor will pass and we will all get used to a new norm, one which involves a further erosion of liberty and dignity at the hands of the government.

You might blame all this on the inventors of the body scanners because they spent millions of dollars lobbying the government for the contract,[68] but that's not the real cause of

---

67 Jordy Yager, "Next step for tight security could be trains, boats, metro," *The Hill*, Nov. 23, 2010 (http://thehill.com/homenews/administration/130549-next-step-for-body-scanners-could-be-trains-boats-and-the-metro-).

68 Fredreka Schouten, "Body scanner makers doubled lobbying cash over 5 years," *USA Today*, Nov. 23, 2010 (http://www.usatoday.com/news/washington/2010-11-22-scanner-lobby_N.htm). The CEO of the company that manufactures one of these machines was one of President Obama's guests on his recent trip to India. OSI Systems Press Release, "Body Scanner Manufacturer Accompanies Obama on Trip to India," *Public Intelligence*, Nov. 10, 2010 (http://publicintelligence.net/body-scanner-manufacturer-accompanies-obama-on-trip-to-india/). This taxpayer-funded trip reportedly cost $200 million per day, and included a coterie of 3000 people. Press Trust of India, "US to spend $200 mn a day on Obama's Mumbai visit," *NDTV*, Nov. 2, 2010 (http://www.ndtv.com/article/india/us-to-spend-200-mn-a-day-on-obama-s-mumbai-visit-64106). A White House spokesman denied that report, but refused to specify the cost. Chris McGreal, "Claim that Barack

this infringement on our liberty. The real cause is the fact that the government has the power to impose the process on us in the first place. If the government did not have the power, there would be no point lobbying it, and the inventors of that machine would have to find a different market for their product.

On his own, the inventor of this body scanning machine is not a threat to our liberties. In a free country, he can't take pictures through your clothes unless you allow it. It's only because the government has taken control of airline security that you have to submit to the choice of being scanned on the one hand, or sexually assaulted on the other.

In a free country, an airline might install such a machine for travelers who think it's worth it for their security on the airplane. Other travelers would fly with an airline that had other security procedures they preferred. So before you blame lobbying, look at the real cause of the problem.

All is not hopeless. There is a growing segment of the population that refuses to slip into the police state mentality. Some of them call themselves survivalists, or "preppers," and some simply developed self-reliance by their upbringing.

Recently an e-mail that illustrates the intellectual revolution against the police state made its way around the country via the Internet. It contained stunning photographs of a recent blizzard that had practically shut down the state of North Dakota. One of those photos showed a car driving through plowed-out snowdrifts three times as tall as the car.

Here is the text of the e-mail (typos and all):

Obama's India visit will cost $200m a day is 'wildly inflated,'" *The Guardian*, Nov. 4, 2010 (http://www.guardian.co.uk/world/2010/nov/04/barack-obama-india-visit-cost-claim).

Thought you'd like to see this one. Maybe we should make North Dakota the capitol of the U S A.

This text is from a county emergency manager in Minot, North Dakota

Minot Daily News

WEATHER BULLETIN

Up here in the Northern part of North Dakota we just recovered from a Historic event -- may I even say a «Weather Event» of «Biblical Proportions» -- with a historic blizzard of up to 25» inches of snow and winds to 50 MPH that broke trees in half, knocked down utility poles, stranded hundreds of motorists in lethal snow banks, closed ALL roads, isolated scores of communities and cut power to 10's of thousands.

FYI:
Obama did not come.
FEMA did nothing.
No one howled for the government.
No one blamed the government.
No one even uttered an expletive on TV.
Jesse Jackson or Al Sharpton did not visit.
Our Mayor's did not blame Obama or anyone else.
Our Governor did not blame Obama or anyone else either.
CNN, ABC, CBS, FOX, or NBC did not visit - or even report on this category 5 snow storm.
Nobody demanded $2,000 debit cards.
No one asked for a FEMA Trailer House.
No one looted.
Nobody - I mean Nobody demanded the government do something.

Nobody expected the government to do anything either.

No Larry King, No Bill O'Rielly, No Oprah, No Chris Mathews and No Geraldo Rivera.

No Shaun Penn, No Barbara Striesand, No Brad Pitts, No Hollywood types to be found.

Nope, we just melted the snow for water.

Sent out caravans of SUV's to pluck people out of snow engulfed cars.

The truck drivers pulled people out of snow banks and didn't ask for a penny.

Local restaurants made food, and the police and fire departments delivered it to the snow bound families..

Families took in the stranded people - total strangers.

We fired up wood stoves, broke out coal oil lanterns or Coleman lanterns.

We put on an extra layers of clothes because up here it is "Work or Die".

We did not wait for some affirmative action government to get us out of a mess created by being immobilized by a welfare program that trades votes for "sittin' at home" checks.

Even though a Category 5 blizzard of this scale is not usual, we know it can happen and how to deal with it ourselves.

I hope this gets passed on.

Maybe .....
SOME people will get the message ......
The world does Not owe you a living.

Some of the factual claims in the e-mail are false; for example, there was indeed an official request that parts of the state be declared a federal disaster area, in order to qualify for federal disaster relief funds.[69] Thus, it's not fair to characterize the people in North Dakota as more self-reliant than those of Louisiana just on the basis of this comparison. Also, some of the photographs were not even taken in North Dakota.

But the point this widely circulated e-mail does illustrate is that many people admire its claims of self-reliance and rugged individualism. The e-mail evinces a mindset that rejects dependency and helplessness, and there are still people in this country who admire that enough to forward the e-mail to thousands or perhaps millions of people.

Resistance to the police state mentality begins where it resides – in your own mind.

Now let's see what would have happened to Joe and Sarah at the grocery store if they lived in a country governed by principles of liberty, instead of one that robs its own citizens of their humanity.

Shortly after Joe and Sarah left Josh and Ben in the car, a passerby noticed the drop-down video screen in the van. She looked inside and saw the three-year-old and another youngster watching the movie, then went into the grocery store. She sought out the security guard.

"There are two children in a van in the parking lot," she told the guard.

Tremaine Watts took just a moment to assess what she had said. "Are they all right?" he asked.

"They seem to be, but you know... they're not supposed

69 "Snow Comparison," *Snopes*, Jan. 11, 2011 (http://www.snopes.com/katrina/soapbox/snowfall.asp).

to be left out there alone. It's against the law, isn't it?"

Tremaine smiled at her reassuringly. "Thank you for telling me. What kind of van is it?"

She told him.

"I'll look into it, ma'am. Have a good day."

"OK."

She went on to do her shopping, and Tremaine keyed his microphone as he headed out the door. "Kevin, I'm going to check something in the parking lot."

"Copy that," Kevin replied from the security office.

Tremaine found the van. The younger kid was still strapped in his car seat, eating what looked like sliced apples, and the older kid was looking at him.

Tremaine smiled and knocked on the window next to Josh.

Josh pause the movie, but didn't roll down the window.

Still smiling, Tremaine spoke clearly so he could be heard through the closed window. "I'm the security guard here. Are you guys OK?"

"No problem," Josh said. "My parents are shopping, and we just wanted to finish the movie. We're fine."

"OK, go right ahead."

Josh nodded and started the movie again.

Tremaine keyed his mic. "Kevin, I'm going to hang around out here a few minutes. Call me if you need me back inside."

In the security office, Kevin worked the remote-control for one of the parking-lot cameras until he spotted Tremaine.

"Everything OK?" Kevin asked.

"Yeah. Just a couple of kids left in the car. One's about two or three, the other one looks twelve or so. They're fine, but a customer mentioned it. I'll stay out here a few minutes."

"Copy that. Things are quiet in here, so we're good for now."

Some idiots leave helpless infants shut up in the car on 90-degree days, but this was a cloudy, 60-degree day in November, and in Tremaine's judgment, it was not a problem. Nonetheless, he and Kevin both understood that since the lady had reported the matter, if something did happen to the kids the store might find itself in an embarrassing position. The older kid looked responsible enough, so there was little risk, but if Tremaine wasn't needed inside it made sense to keep an eye on things.

Fifteen minutes later, Joe and Sarah were pushing their buggy full of groceries to the van. Tremaine was pacing in the next parking aisle.

Joe spotted him.

Tremaine smiled and waved. "Have a good day, sir."

Joe waved back.

Once in the driver's seat, Joe asked Josh about the guard.

"Yeah, he came over a few minutes ago," Josh said. "Just checking on us."

"That's nice," Sarah said.

"What's for supper?" Josh asked.

"Possum stew," Joe said. Sarah slapped his leg. "I mean, your mom's delicious ragout."

21

CRISIS AND THE
CONSOLIDATION OF POWER

Rahm Emmanuel, President Obama's former White House Chief of Staff, openly acknowledged the political utility of crises when he said that "you never want a serious crisis to go to waste. And what I mean by that, it's an opportunity to do things you think you could not do before."[70] He was talking about the economic meltdown following the subprime mortgage crisis, and how it represented an opportunity for the government to accomplish things that were impossible unless the population was in a panic.

Congress responded by passing the so-called economic stimulus bill, "a political wonder that manages to spend money on just about every pent-up Democratic proposal of the last 40 years."[71] The published cost was a sum so huge it boggles the mind – $787 billion – but none of the cooler heads actually believed we'd get off that cheap. The true figure is at least $3.2 trillion,[72] and the irony is that it only

---

70 WSJDigitalNetwork, (Rahm Emanuel on the Opportunities of Crisis," http://www. youtube.com/watch?v=_mzcbXi1Tkk (Nov. 19, 2008).

71 "A 40-Year Wish List," *The Wall Street Journal*, Jan. 28, 2009 (http://online.wsj.com/ article/SB123310466514522309.html).

72 Conn Carroll, "True Cost of Stimulus: $3.27 Trillion," The Foundry, Feb. 12, 2009

worsened the economic situation. But fixing something was never the government's goal – its goal was to gobble up more or our liberties.

When people are in their right mind they know that it's dangerous and foolish to let the government nationalize industries, expand welfare policies, and control gazillions of dollars. But when there's a crisis, Rahm is saying, now you can churn up panic. The government can put on its cape and leggings and come to the rescue. "Have no fear! We're from the government, and we're here to help!" Before you know it, you've wasted more money and lost more liberty.

The fact that this is all a big joke is dramatically illustrated by a video in which President Obama and a pack of crony capitalists get a big laugh at the fact that the "stimulus" failed to stimulate the economy.[73] When you watch this, note how they laugh about how they pulled off the scam.

Assuming nothing more than a politician's self-interest, economic theory predicts that in a democratic system he will redistribute (or promise to redistribute) more than his opponent in order to win the next election, so it's in his interest to spend the most money he can, regardless of the long term havoc. During a crisis, voters get this feeling that "somebody's gotta do something," but they themselves don't have the power to do it. Now here comes a politician who says "we're from the government. We're going to solve your problem." The voter feels relieved, and hands over the power to act.

Unfortunately, the politician never solves the problem. All he does is use fear as an opportunity to tax more, spend

---

(http://blog.heritage.org/2009/02/12/true-cost-of-stimulus-327-trillion/).

73 ThinkFY, "Obama: Shovel-Ready Not as Shovel-Ready as We Expected," http://youtu.be/O55aRrvXtio (June 13, 2011).

more, redistribute more wealth, and gain more power than he could have before the crisis.

It's easy to see that the government has an incentive to take advantage of crises, and in fact to manufacture them.

News outlets routinely collude with the government to manufacture crises, which provides ongoing opportunities to prey on fear-driven public demands for government action. The BP oil spill comes to mind (calls to stop drilling in the Gulf), as does every weather event and natural phenomenon that can be related to global warming (calls to reduce emissions and energy consumption and impose a "carbon tax"), the tsunami that hit Japan in 2011 (calls to stop nuclear power development), the Tuscon shooting of 2011 (calls for more gun control laws), the food poisoning outbreaks that happen almost every year (calls for more FDA power). I could go on for literally dozens of pages.

None of these crises ever result in a reduction in the size of government, lower tax rates, fewer regulations, or more liberty in any respect whatsoever. But neither do these crises ever go away for long; the government's action never actually solves anything.

22

SNAPSHOTS OF VARIOUS GOVERNMENT ACTIVITIES

Anti Price-Gouging Laws

After Japan's Tsunami of 2011, there was a rush on potassium iodide tablets in the United States.[74] Most outlets sold out two or three days after the US Surgeon General recommended that people buy it, and those that still had some for sale had raised the price enormously. A two-week supply of potassium iodide that normally cost about $12 was available on eBay for $499.

After Hurricane Katrina, John Sheperson heard that people in Mississippi were out of electricity and needed generators, so he bought 19 of them, drove to Mississippi, and offered them for sale for twice the price he had paid.

People get outraged when they hear stories like these, and demand that the government "do something." (To find out what happened to John Sheperson and his generators, read *Mississippi Has a Place for Heroes: Jail* at http://www. realclearpolitics.com/articles/2006/05/mississippi_has_a_ place_for_he.html).

---

74 Andrew Pollack, Anxiety Over Radiation Drives a Sales Surge for a Drug Against Thyroid Cancer," *The New York Times*, March 15, 2011 (http://www.nytimes. com/2011/03/16/health/16iodide.html).

What these people fail to understand is that market-driven high prices are good because they relieve shortages and direct things where they are needed, better than government rationing. These initial high prices attract competition – a bigger supply of goods – which drives prices down. Note also that high pricing spreads the wealth in a natural way, as opposed to a socialistic way; wealthier people buy the goods at high price, in essence subsidizing the arrival of more goods at falling prices so poorer people can afford them as well.

If someone really is taking unfair advantage of the situation (price-gouging), someone else will see an opportunity to gain customers by offering the same goods at a lower price. The problem is solved without throwing anyone in jail and perpetuating the shortage. So if you have a moral objection to price-gouging, you're saying the seller actually has a reasonable opportunity to sell at a lower price, and it's your duty to prove it by providing the goods at a reasonable price.

But, of course, those very people who complain have less incentive to provide the goods; by their own argument they have priced themselves below the market, proving the lie of their "price-gouging" accusation. They don't actually provide the goods at lower prices; instead they run to the government to have the seller arrested, and no one gets the goods.

But the stupidity of government apparently knows no bounds; anti-price-gouging policies actually cause more price-gouging. It's a fundamental principle of economics that you get more of whatever you're subsidizing. If you subsidize corn production, you'll get more corn. If you subsidize unemployment, you'll get more unemployment. If you subsidize illegitimacy, you'll get more illegitimate children.

Anti-gouging laws are a subsidy. They subsidize a lack of foresight and preparedness. "Price gouging" usually occurs in disaster or emergency situations; this offensively high pricing of goods encourages foresight, planning, and wise preparation so you don't put yourself at the mercy of someone with an emergency-induced opportunity to take advantage of your need by raising prices.

Anti-gouging laws subsidize a lack of preparedness, so that's exactly what you'll get more of and, as a result, you'll have more price-gouging when the next disaster strikes.

Rent Controls

Rent controls are just a variety of anti-gouging laws; they put a legal limit on how much a landlord can charge for an apartment, and this results in shortages. Rents respond to supply and demand – the more people there are who want an apartment, the higher the price will be, which attracts the production of more apartments, which means there are more apartments to rent, which drives the price down.

Limiting the amount of rent the landlord can charge means that the landlord will not build more apartments. New people needing apartments will not be able to find any. Thus, rent controls lead to shortages.

Rent control is also a kind of subsidy – by rewarding people for having low incomes, it subsidizes, and therefore perpetuates, low incomes.

Public Employment

Government "services" are a special kind of economic good. Take, for instance, the case of public teachers. They do produce something, and there are costs associated with what they do, but no one buys it in a market. We don't purchase government services. The government takes our money by force and then gives us public education, or whatever, whether we like it or not.

Because there is no market for the product or service, it has no value in the economic sense, only in the political sense and, because it has no value, it is provided without any regard for its quality (which can't be priced anyway). In other words, providing a better education incurs no profit, and a bad one no penalty.[75] The government employee's salary is not tied to how good a service is provided – it remains the same or even increases regardless of quality. This simply subsidizes bad performance, laziness, long lines, arrogance, and demagoguery of the kind we saw in Wisconsin ("you're trying to starve hardworking middle-class Americans" – this from people who earned about twice as much as their private-sector counterparts).

Have you ever noticed how public employees are almost always in favor of higher tax rates? It's because they don't pay taxes; they're actually net tax beneficiaries.

Look at it this way: If you earn $50,000 a year and pay $10,000, your take-home pay is 80% of your salary. But if we cut taxes to zero, your take-home pay goes up to 100% of your salary. If your money in hand increases when we cut taxes to zero, it's because you are a net payer of taxes.

With a public employee it's a whole different story: If he earns $50,000 a year and we cut taxes to zero, his take-home pay will be 0% of his salary because he will lose his job. This

---

75 Yes, some individual public teachers work hard to provide a good education because of their good moral character, and in that sense they reap an altruistic profit, but I'm talking about the irresistible forces of economics and their ultimate effect on the quality and nature of government services. To those teachers who are not cynically careless of their teaching duties, I would just point out that public education by its very nature is harmful to children, families, and civilization in general, because it discourages parental involvement in their child's upbringing, thereby bringing on a decline in the quality of families in society. So, however well they may do their teaching job, their very participation in the public education system is harmful to us all.

shows that he's a net recipient of taxes, not a net payer.[76] In other words, one hundred percent of his take-home pay is a subsidy (net government handout).

Here's another way to look at it. Suppose the government starts with $1,000,000 in its fund. Jack Baker earns $100,000 in his bakery and pays $30,000 in taxes. At the end of his dealings with the government, the public fund has increased by $30,000 to a total of $1,030,000.

Now let's start again with $1,000,000, but this time we're looking at Bob Justice, a government-paid judge. He also earned $100,000 from the government and paid $30,000 in taxes. But at the end of his transaction with the government, the public fund has decreased by $70,000 to a total of $930,000. The government didn't gain any money by "collecting taxes" from Bob Justice as it did when it collected from Jack Baker; it actually lost money.

Why? Because Bob Justice isn't really a tax payer, but a tax consumer.[77] Paying him $100,000 and then taking back $30,000 is just an accounting trick to fool people into thinking he pays taxes.

Welfare

We don't have real poverty in America, unless it is self-inflicted by drug abuse or alcoholism. Wherever you find abject poverty in the world – the kind that kills – the cause is always government. The reason it has been absent from America is because prosperity is one of the natural blessings of liberty. My grandparents were much poorer than today's "poor," but

---

76 Hoppe, *Democracy: The God that Failed,* 100.

77 The fact that a state government might pay the salary and the federal government collect the tax is irrelevant, because that is merely a bookkeeping entry in the transaction between one level of government and another, both of whom contribute to the salaries of public employees in the form of grants and direct subsidies.

they never resented anyone because of it. The so-called poor are actually quite wealthy, just less wealthy than those who are wealthier. We do use the term "poor," but it's a political description, not an economic one, and in that sense poverty exists in America, as it does anywhere, only because of the state. Look at the poorest cities in America and there you'll find the most intensive involvement of the state in the form of welfare programs. The term "poor" describes those who are on the receiving end of wealth redistribution programs.

Instead of running to the government to solve the poverty problem, we should have championed liberty first and let good people come to the aid of those in need. Private charities and civic organizations are far more effective in dealing with poverty than the government. In fact, government welfare programs perpetuate poverty. Politicians have every incentive to keep poor people poor. People on welfare want to keep getting their free money, so they vote for politicians who promise to keep giving it to them. Recall our observation that whatever the state profits from, it will act so as to create more of it. What is welfare but a subsidy of poverty? And whatever you subsidize, you get more of it.

Indeed, today there are more people on welfare than ever before. In 2010, there were more than 42 million people receiving food stamps.[78] That's nearly 14% of the population of the United States. Washington, DC, the seat of the federal government, had the highest rate: 21.1% of the population.

It's astounding to consider that more than one-third – 35% – of all income in the US is a direct wealth-transfer in the form of welfare benefits.[79] Look at it this way; of all the income

---

78 Sara Murray, "In U.S., 14% Rely on Food Stamps," *The Wall Street Journal*, Nov. 4, 2010 (http://blogs.wsj.com/economics/2010/11/04/some-14-of-us-uses-food-stamps/).

79 John Mellowy, "Welfare State: Handouts Make Up One-Third of U.S. Wages,"

people receive in the United States, 35% of that money is simply taken from taxpayers and given to the recipients, and that doesn't even count the money "earned" by government employees, which is also a direct wealth-transfer.

Even more mind-boggling is the fact that the amount of money handed out in this process now exceeds tax revenues.[80]

Private charities are not like the government in how they handle welfare. In order to survive, they have to be responsible with their charity, otherwise people stop making contributions. When people on public welfare use their welfare debit cards to gamble in Las Vegas and buy cruise ship tickets, nothing changes. But the recipients of private charity will lose their income if they abuse it.

Politicians scoff at the idea of holding welfare recipients accountable; they call it hard-hearted and unkind, even while they take your money and dispense it against your will.

What if you don't believe in a particular government charity program? Tough; you have to contribute anyway. In 2009, Planned Parenthood received several hundred million dollars of your taxes, and performed more than 300,000 abortions. Even if you believe a woman should be free to choose an abortion, I'm pretty sure that deep down you can't honestly justify taking my money by force to pay for it.

Meanwhile, it is a federal crime to destroy bald eagle eggs, and the government spends tax money prosecuting human beings to protect bird eggs. This upside-down sense of right and wrong is typical of government thinking.

CNBC, Mar. 8, 2011 (http://www.cnbc.com/id/41969508/).

80 Elizabeth MacDonald, "Government Cash Handouts Now Top Tax Revenues," *Fox News*, April 10, 2011 (http://www.foxbusiness.com/markets/2011/04/20/government-cash-handouts-exceed-tax-revenues/).

There is a better way. In a free country, you are free to dispense charity as you see fit. Charities compete for your contributions by being the most responsible with the funds and being the most effective at addressing whatever social ill concerns them.

In a free country, if you think it's important to save a rare desert toad, you are free to persuade others to pool their money to buy a tract of land in their habitat and protect it. As it is, the government spends your money protecting those toads whether you like it or not. The government doesn't use persuasion; it uses force. If you don't pay the taxes spent on these programs, the government will come with guns and put you in a concrete cell.

23

THE REASON FOR WAR[81]

Hitler and Tojo were some of the most evil people in history. In World War II the German government was responsible for nearly 21 million murders, and the Japanese nearly 6 million. This does not include people killed in combat – this is the number of non-fighting citizens murdered by their own governments.[82]

In the United States, people said something must be done, and so the US government allied itself with Stalin, who was fighting Hitler. The only problem is that Stalin murdered more than twice as many as Hitler, a total of 42.7 million.[83] From the end of the war until their loss of power in the 1990s, by conservative estimates the Soviets went on to murder an additional 20 million people, not counting those killed in armed conflicts.[84] This was our ally. If murder made Hitler a bad guy, then Stalin was worse.

Now let's look at the Japanese and their enemy the Chinese. In World War II the Japanese murdered more than

---

81 I wish to thank Richard Maybury for his excellent book on this subject, *World War II: The Rest Of The Story,* (Placerville: Bluestocking Press, 2003).

82 R.J. Rummel, *Death by Government* (New Brunswick: Transaction Publishers, 1994).

83 Id.

84 Id.

5.9 million people, but we sided with the Chinese leader Chiang Kai-Shek, who murdered more than 10 million.

Clearly, we didn't choose our allies based on how good they were to their own citizens. Maybe there was some other reason. You were probably taught in school that Hitler had to be stopped because he wanted to conquer the world. But look at an atlas from the early 1940s and you'll find that Hitler never commanded more than 4% of the world at a time when the Soviets had already conquered 16%.

Moreover, the Germans never had the military capability to beat the British, because they didn't have the Higgins boat. That's the boat you've seen in movie reels of the great D-Day invasion at Normandy. It's basically a rectangular bathtub that drops a ramp when the boat hits the beach, and the troops jump out firing. Without this boat, the Germans couldn't invade England. They would have had to capture a port to unload their troops, and a port is a lot easier to defend than miles and miles of beach.

Hitler's generals were well aware of their military weakness, and advised him not to start a fight with anyone. What we call the Battle of Britain was a long bombing raid, not an invasion. It's well-known in military circles that you need air support for an invasion, but you can't invade with air support alone. Just look what happened after a few months of the Battle of Britain; when it became clear that he could not beat the British, Hitler decided to invade Russia.

From that moment, he was doomed. You see, you can't invade Russia. They have an invincible force on their side – winter. When an army invades, the Russians simply retreat mile-by-mile and wait for winter. When the invading army's equipment gets bogged down in snow, mud, and ice, their extremely long, thin supply lines dry up. That's when the

Russians attack. General Kutuzov defeated Napoleon this way, and it's how the Russians defeated Hitler.

None of this was a big surprise to our politicians and military leaders. It's not something that only recently came to light with the benefit of hindsight. "Never invade Russia" is just about the first thing soldiers learn in military school, right after "Don't attack your main suppliers," and Hitler did both.[85] He depended on the Soviets for oil and rubber, and when he attacked them his supply was cut off.

I know you're looking for a rational explanation for Hitler's stupidity, and there actually is one; he was insane. Seriously, there's nothing more to it than that. In the several thousand years of recorded wars, the only one ever to successfully invade Russia was Genghis Khan, and it took him four years to do it. Hitler was a military idiot with no concept of logistics, which is kind of redundant to say; to get into a military conflict without understanding logistics is idiotic.[86]

Hitler never stood a chance against the British or the Russians, and the idea that this stupid amateur might take over the world was laughable. Yes, it was the subject of a lot of World War II propaganda, and in that day I'm sure a lot of good people fell for it because they had faith in their government, but today there's no excuse for believing that. Clearly the Soviets were a lot more serious about (and more capable of) taking over the world. So if stopping murderous villains hellbent on conquering the world was the reason to make war, then we should really have allied with Hitler to fight Stalin.

---

85 Martin van Creveld, *Supplying War*, (Cambridge: Cambridge University Press, 1977).

86 This is why military historians have the pithy saying, "amateurs focus on strategy; experts focus on logistics."

———— ⊗⊗⊗ ————

This leads to an interesting question: Why *did* we fight in World War II?

It wasn't to stop Hitler from taking over the world – he couldn't do it, and our own ally Stalin was a much bigger threat in that respect.

It wasn't because Hitler was the most murderous villain – Stalin was at the very least twice as murderous.

Then why?

To understand, you have to do something very strange – you have to think like a politician. Put yourself in the position of one of our rulers. What do these people do? They govern. They rule other people. They determine how we should live, but they don't live by the limitations they impose on us. They take our money at gunpoint and use it for whatever purposes they devise. They live by special privileges that we don't have. Their whole purpose in life is to dominate others.

Well, the ultimate form of domination is to kill, and the grandest way to kill is to mobilize the force and productivity of an entire nation against another. The use of force, especially military force, is the most exciting exercise of political power, and politicians rarely pass up the opportunity to use it. In all the whirlwind rush of power they have, this is the biggest, most addictive rush of all.

And so we have wars.

Naturally, these people, the politicians, don't just go around telling us we need to fight wars because it's great fun. They tell us it's to stop a mass-murdering villain, or to stop someone from taking over the world, or maybe to liberate some oppressed people in another country.

Or maybe they talk about our "national interests." Have you ever wondered what a "national interest" is? Politicians are never very clear about those, but from context you can kind of figure out what they're talking about.

In the Gulf war our "national interests" were maybe protecting Kuwait from invasion by Iraq, so then I ask myself, am I willing to send my son to die in Kuwait to stop Iraqis from invading? Do I care so much about it that I'm willing for my son to die? Or maybe it was to make sure we kept a steady supply of oil from Iraq – again, do I want their oil so urgently that I'll sacrifice my life or my son's, or maybe your son's?

What about liberating the Iraqi people themselves? Is that worth the life of my son or yours? I'm sympathetic to the plight of oppressed people all over the world, but honestly I'm not interested in letting my son die to liberate them, and you most certainly have no right to send him against his will. If our rulers feel so strongly about their cause, let them fight the battle themselves.

If we're to be in the business of liberating all the oppressed people of the world, we'll never stop fighting. It's better to secure a stronghold of liberty here in our country and invite the poor, the downtrodden, those huddled masses yearning to be free, to come here. If we're talking about defending that, our own country, our own territory, our own liberty, that's a different matter.

That's something I'd fight for.

There is another reason for war that we can't simply ignore – there's a lot of money involved. The US military has been active somewhere almost constantly for the last hundred years, and since World War II the interventions have become ever larger and more expensive. The money spent on the war machine doesn't just get blown up; it is given to defense contractors. The bombs might explode in a desert somewhere, but the money to buy them was transferred from taxpayers to bomb-builders.

And the sums are staggering. Every day at 5 p.m. the US Department of Defense publishes the contracts awarded that day if they exceed $5 million. The total is often over a billion dollars, and it's rarely less than a hundred million per day. See for yourself: http://www.defense.gov/contracts/default.aspx.

Because the government subsists on tax dollars, assuming nothing more than self-interest on the part of government agents you have to expect them always to find ways to increase taxes. One way to do this, as we've seen, is to manufacture demand for the services the government provides, so that it can use the increased "need" as justification to increase taxes.

Consider state-run security in light of this principle. The government is our sole provider of national security. If there is nothing for an army to do, there's no point having it sit around doing nothing, so you reduce the size of the army and send people home. The military budget decreases. But if there are threats, then you can mobilize this army and put it to use. The budget increases. Procurements rise. Defense contractors get rich, and retiring politicians find a home on their boards of directors. The retired politician has connections back in the government; he gets ever more money for the defense contractor, who gets even richer.

The only thing needed to kickstart this warfare-state apparatus is a national security threat of some kind, anything that will make citizens demand that we go somewhere far away and kick butt. The pressure to find excuses of this kind is enormous, and so, unsurprisingly, you'll find no shortage of them. Where you have a demand, someone will supply.

Sometimes the politicians just get lucky and a provocation lands in their lap. But sometimes we have to wonder if they aren't the ones doing the provoking. Remember, whenever the state profits from an activity, it will cause this activity to take place so it can profit from it even more. The existence of welfare programs means that politicians profit from poverty, so we see a historical increase in what we call "poverty." The state profits from crime because it creates a great demand for policing and judicial services, and so today we have the highest incarceration rate in our history.[87]

Similarly, to the extent the state profits from war, you can be certain it will act so as to increase the incidence of war. It might be "trigger-happy," overreacting to external provocations. Or it might deliberately provoke others into supplying an "incident" that requires a response, as we did in Panama in 1989. Or the government might learn that an incident is about to happen, but do nothing to stop it because it needs the excuse to enter an ongoing war – Pearl Harbor. Worst of all, we can't simply discount the possibility that interested parties on our side might create the incident themselves and blame it on a boogieman. There is recent precedent for this; Project Gunrunner. In 2010 the Bureau of Alcohol, Tobacco, and Firearms deliberately allowed the illegal sale of guns to Mexican drug cartels so it could complain about American guns getting into the hands of the drug cartels and demand more gun control. Conspiracy theories are fun to scoff at, because so many of them are kooky, but anyone who is just moderately wise about human nature will understand why these things happen. You'll find it hard to believe that Americans like us would do such things, but you must remember that our rulers are not like us. They're very, very different. We would never rule anyone; we would guarantee their liberty.

---

87 This is despite the fact that violent crime has decreased since the mid-1990s, possibly due to a resurgence at the State level of the right to carry concealed weapons. The government has simply shifted its focus to non-violent crimes.

Terrorism has been a simply fabulous warmonger. Whoever came up with that idea is a genius. You have a nameless, nationless enemy who is everywhere except here, so you can fight him all over the world while the domestic population goes on about its business, pretty much oblivious to the bombing. You're not fighting a nation per se, because the terrorist is embedded, so you can fight him without fighting an organized military force and suffering politically undesirable casualties. The terrorist is secretive and hidden, so you don't know who he is and you never really know if he's dead yet, and you can just keep fighting him forever. It never has to end!

The War on Terror's collateral benefits to the state in terms of power and taxation are essentially limitless. The United States has engaged in a total war on terrorism since 2001, resulting in a totalitarian national security apparatus. We have a new Department of Homeland Security, an internal assault on our own liberties by passage of the USA PATRIOT Act, oppressive and physically intrusive security measures for air travel and a trend now underway toward extending them to all modes of public transportation, the complete abolition of financial privacy, and so on.

Exercising all this power takes vast amounts of money. As of mid-2011 the federal government was spending well over $10,000,000,000 (ten billion dollars) per day, or $120,000 per second.

And so now we have a more complete understanding of what has always been the reason for war: power and money.

24

IS THERE A POLITICAL
SOLUTION?

We tend to see politics as lying on a spectrum that spans from liberalism on one end to conservatism on the other end.[88] Liberals are on the left, and conservatives are on the right. Democrats are liberals/leftists, and Republicans are conservatives/rightists.

Democrat/Left   **Republican/Right**

Political Spectrum

Socialism   **Fascism**

That's pretty much the simple overview, but this explanation leaves out some very important things. First and most importantly, the typical view of politics doesn't contain a "liberty factor." That is, socialism and fascism are equally horrendous infringements on liberty. On this chart, liberty

---

88 A complete study of the political parties and their influence is beyond the scope of this chapter. Thanks to Richard J. Maybury for his clarity of thinking on this issue; many of the ideas in this chapter are developed from his excellent book, *Are You Liberal? Conservative? or Confused?* (Placerville: Bluestocking Press, 2004).

is equally at risk no matter which party is in control... so where's the "free" end of the spectrum? It doesn't exist; we have to create one.

If you make a chart showing where conservatives and liberals land on the issue of liberty, you'll find that they're both on the wrong end of the spectrum. They both want the government to encroach on your liberties; they only differ as to the reason for the encroachment.

In general, liberals want encroachment in economic matters and they want liberty in social matters, whereas republicans want the opposite. But neither one of them wants liberty in all areas.

	Want Liberty	**Want Encroachment**
Liberals	Drug use Pornography Sexual preference Prostitution	Taxes for wealth transfers Gun control Wage and price controls Medical care Labor unions
Conservatives	Taxes for wealth transfers Gun control Wage and price controls Medical care Labor unions	Drug use Pornography Sexual preference Prostitution

Liberals and Conservatives both infringe our liberties.

As you can see, liberals want liberty in sexual conduct, and conservatives want liberty primarily in matters, but neither one takes a hard line for liberty in all areas.

So-called centrists or moderates are no friends of liberty. In fact, they are the worst of all, for they want encroachment in social *and* economic matters. They could have staked out a central position by rejecting encroachment in all things, but instead they defined themselves as centrists by accepting regulation of all conduct.

One thing I need to make clear: By rejecting government encroachment in all areas of life, liberty-minded people do not advocate poverty and sexual perversion. It's just that we prefer non-governmental solutions to social and economic issues, because the government can address these issues only by infringing our liberties, and even then it never solves the problem. Voluntary (non-governmental) solutions are more effective and preserve our liberties.

Take a look again at the issues in the chart above. The American founders believed that the federal government had no business with any of these issues, and nowhere in the Constitution will you find a grant of power allowing the federal government to regulate them.

But as we have seen, the Constitution doesn't bind the government anymore.

Washington Post columnist Ezra Klein typifies the liberal view of the Constitution. He says that it "has no binding power on anything" and is "confusing because it was written more than a hundred years ago."[89] This contempt for the Constitution pervades the media and the government, because it is an obstacle to their desire to rule.

The Republicans don't affirmatively state such contempt, and actually pay lip-service to the Constitution, but when it comes to making difficult choices such as opposing unconstitutional power-grabs, they're as useless as the democrats.

---

89 Larry O'Connor, "Which Part of the Constitution is 'Confusing' Ezra?" *Big Journalism,* Dec. 30, 2010 (http://bigjournalism.com/sright/2010/12/30/which-part-of-the-constitution-is-confusing-ezra/).

To compound the problem, we live in a two-party system. What that means is that a statist minority can rule the country, even when a majority of the people prefer liberty.

It works like this: In an election you might have 40% socialist voters, 30% weakly conservative voters, and 30% strongly conservative voters. So 60% of the people oppose socialism, but they're split; the weak conservatives oppose socialism but support big government for various purposes, while the strong conservatives strongly oppose socialism and big government in general. (These people are often libertarians and don't realize it. Libertarians are ultra-conservative on the issue of federal power, in that they oppose the power of central government even more strongly than conservatives do). On election day, the strong and weak liberty-oriented voters divide their votes, and the socialists win the day. That's what happened in the 1992 presidential election; George H.W. Bush and Ross Perot split the conservative vote, and Clinton won.

We had a similar situation in 2008, except there was no viable third candidate. John McCain was a RINO (Republican in name only) par excellence. As a candidate, he was merely bad from a conservative standpoint, but for voters who are actually conscious of the assault on their liberties, he was a disaster. Like a lot of people in the Republican party leadership, he was perceived as "spineless" when it came to defending the concept of liberty. As a consequence, he failed to generate much support. While a lot of conservatives and libertarians voted against Obama, many of them were disgusted with the republican candidate and fed up with republican failures in general; enough of them stayed home on election day to hand Obama a victory.

I have spoken to some of the voters who stayed home, and most of them told me they thought McCain was worse than George W. Bush, the outgoing president, and they were already fed up with him and his policies. They now admit that Obama has done even worse than they expected from McCain, but their position is that the two choices were so bad that it didn't matter. These voters are no longer willing to support a bad Republican candidate just to avoid a Democratic one who is a little worse, because that keeps rewarding the Republican party for fielding bad candidates.

If anything, these people feel that if both parties are taking the country to hell anyway, we might as well get it over with and start over. By this way of thinking, we're better off voting for the socialist Democrats so we can go ahead and destroy the country. The sooner that happens, the sooner we can start with a clean slate.

Not everyone feels this way, of course, so the Republicans hold themselves out as a less destructive option. They don't expressly describe themselves that way, of course, but the Libertarians see it that way. One of the stay-at-home voters I spoke to said it's as if the Republicans are trying to see how badly they can behave and still get elected.

Actually, that's exactly what's going on.

Remember that politicians love power more than anything else. The leaders in the republican party are interested in conservative principles only to the extent that their interest keeps getting them elected. Mostly what they're interested in is maintaining the ability to exercise power. If saying stuff that sounds conservative allows them to do that, then fine, they'll say that or whatever else it takes.

The democrats are the expert power-grabbers, and their policies grow the government and its power more than republican policies do. But when republicans see this, it makes them envious – they wish they had that much power, and so they start trending more toward democrat socialist policies, where the real power is. They move as far from conservative principles as they can and still get elected, but sometimes they miscalculate.

That's what happened in the 2008 election with McCain. He represents the so-called moderate or centrist politician who takes neither a strong conservative position, nor a strong liberal one. Moderates could have distinguished themselves by advocating liberty in all areas, but instead they define their centrist position by advocating liberty in none. Of course, this makes sense; they're hungry for power, and granting liberty to everyone would leave them no one to rule.

It seems a quandary. If we're going to win our liberties back by the political process, we have to elect people who don't want political power; people who will dismantle the federal power structure once in office, knowing they will then spend the rest of their time not governing anyone.

Those people are hard to find, for two reasons. First, political power is inherently wicked; it is, after all, the power to use force against people who have done you no harm. That's why the founders denied much political power to the federal government in the first place. So we have to elect people who will use that power only for the purpose of removing it from the government. How can you be sure they won't be seduced by that power once they have it? All the historical evidence shows that, while there are a very few people who maintain their integrity in office, there are too few of them to keep the government as a whole from growing out of control.

Secondly, the people most likely to resist the seduction of power are usually not interested in running for office. The last thing they want to do is deal on a daily basis with crooked politicians, demagogues, and the institutionalized criminality of government.

The Tea Party's idea is that as between the two main parties, the Republican Party has more of an affinity with the concepts of liberty. It's grassroots strategy is to topple the power-hungry leadership in the Republican Party, take control of the government, and dismantle its power structure.

It's an ambitious and difficult program, and it stands a better chance than the formation of a third party, which would only split the conservatives into two losing minority groups. But if the Republican leadership doesn't change its ways, the Tea Party will not hesitate to form a third party, because they firmly believe they can succeed. They think they represent a majority of thinking in the country – the only question is whether it's a large enough majority to remain bigger than the liberal Democrats when die-hard moderate Republicans refuse to join them.

The RINOs being what they are, they'll join the Democrats before they cede control to the Tea Party. We saw them completely betray us in the so-called Debt Ceiling Crisis of 2011. The Tea Party Republicans in the House passed a bill that would have required a balanced budget and substantial spending cuts before authorizing an increase in the national debt, but the old-guard Republicans in the Senate undermined their efforts and sided with Democrats to pass a bill that increased the debt, increased spending by *trillions* of dollars, and created an unconstitutional Super Congress that will do nothing but sap more liberties away from us.

To succeed, the Tea Partiers will have to gain control of the House of Representatives, the Senate, and the Presidency, and then they'll have to maintain the discipline to abolish many of the government programs and agencies on which the citizens are now dependent.

Doing so will be difficult. Even before the debt ceiling fiasco we saw the Republican party leadership's enormous resistance to the Tea Party's attempts to reduce government spending. A campaign pledge to cut $100 billion from the 2011 budget was whittled down to a nominal $38 billion, bet even this figure was a sham. After looking through the accounting tricks, the real reduction was only $352 million, and if you include "emergency spending" outlays it will actually result in a budget increase of more than $3 billion over 2010.[90] In Washington, you can increase spending and call it a budget cut.

But even if you take the $38 billion at face value, it's insignificant in terms of a budget cut. The government is running a deficit of $1.56 trillion per year,[91] which means that it added $38 billion to the national debt in the 9 days preceding the vote on the "budget cuts." In that light, $38 billion in cuts is not impressive at all, and yet this pitiful sum was the biggest federal budget cut in history.

Clearly something drastic needs to be done in order to achieve meaningful cuts in government spending, but there's nothing like that on the horizon. Even the Tea Party's own ten-year budget plan doesn't theoretically balance the budget until 2040,[92] which means, of course, that it has a deficit every

---

90 Tim Fernhoz, "CBO Says Budget Deal Will Cut Spending by Only $352 Million This Year," *National Journal*, April 14, 2011 (http://www.nationaljournal.com/budget/cbo-says-budget-deal-will-cut-spending-by-only-352-million-this-year-20110413).

91 Alister Bull and Jeff Mason, "Obama's 2010 budget: deficit soars amid job spending," *Reuters*, Feb. 1, 2010 (http://www.reuters.com/article/2010/02/01/idUSN31157907). Actually, the rate was over $1.6 trillion per year during the first two years of Obama administration leading up to this budget deal. Terence P. Jeffrey, "Federal Borrowing on Pace to Hit Debt Limit in Less Than Week," *CNSNews.com*, April 20, 2011 (http://www. cnsnews.com/news/article/federal-borrowing-pace-hit-debt-limit-le).

92 Erik Wasson and Pete Kasperowicz, "House passes Ryan's '12 budget; conservatives want more cuts," *The Hill*, April 15, 2011 (http://thehill.com/blogs/on-the-money/budget/156379-house-clears-ryans-2012-budget-plan-conservatives-want-more-cuts).

year until then, increasing the debt burden on you and your children anyway. The plan is just a House budget resolution, not a bill, so even if the Senate approved it, it still would never become law.

In sum, even after a Tea Party landslide in 2010, we still don't have anything resembling fiscal sanity in Washington. If $38 billion in cuts is the best we can expect, especially when they actually amount to yet another spending increase, the Tea Party will have to look somewhere other than the Republican Party for a set of principles that will save the country.

Fortunately, there is one other option.

25

THE GREAT LIBERTARIAN
ERROR: ABORTION

I have been urged to avoid the term "libertarian" to keep
from alienating my conservative audience. Yes, it comes
with a lot of baggage, but we have to get over it. When I
travel overseas I get saddled with a stereotype that comes
from being an "American;" imperialistic, domineering,
ignorant, and so on, all of which are characteristics of the
US government, not of Americans citizens per se. But what
else should I call myself? I'm grateful to be an American; our
nation was founded on liberty, and was a beacon of liberty
in a dark world. We need to embrace the concept of liberty,
think in terms of liberty, be grateful for God-given liberty,
defend it, recover it, and establish it, and let the blessings of
liberty shine for all the world to see. What else do you call
this liberty-oriented mindset but "libertarian?"

As the great libertarian Hans-Hermann Hoppe observes,
there is a natural, substantive affinity between conservatism
and libertarianism. He describes the modern conservative as

someone who believes in the natural existence of a
natural order, a natural state of affairs which corresponds
to the nature of things... who recognizes the old and
natural through the "noise" of anomalies and accidents

and who defends, supports, and helps to preserve it against the temporary and anomalous....

Conservatives,... if they stand for anything, stand for and want to preserve the family and the social hierarchies and layers of material as well as spiritual-intellectual authority based on and growing out of family bonds and kinship relations.[93]

Statism is inherently antagonistic to conservatism, because "the family disintegration and moral and cultural decay which contemporary conservatives deplore is largely the result of the erosion and destruction of households (estates) as the economic basis of families by the modern welfare state."[94] Thus, a principled conservative should be consistently anti-statist, for as we have seen, in a democracy the state always seizes social welfare power.[95]

Conversely, the principled libertarian must be consistently conservative.[96] Conservatism and libertarianism focus on two sides of the same coin:

[O]n the one hand families, kinship relations, communities, authority and social hierarchy, and on the other hand property and its appropriation, transformation and transfer.... Extensively, that is, their realm of inquiry (frame of reference) is identical. Families, authority, communities, and social ranks are the empirical-sociological concretization of the abstract philosophical-praxeological categories and concepts of property, production, ex-

---

93 Hoppe, *Democracy: The God That Failed*, 187-188.

94 Id. at 203.

95 See ch. 17, *The American Form of Government*.

96 Indeed, most of the leading libertarian thinkers were social-cultural conservatives. See Hoppe, *Democracy: The God That Failed*, 202.

change, and contract. Property and property relations do not exist apart from families and kinship relations.[97]

In other words, stateless governance takes place within the social structure erected on the foundation of the family unit – the clan, tribe, community, and "nation." No stateless libertarian society can endure without conserving the stable, normal, functional, morally-grounded family household as the basis of all social and cultural hierarchies.

The unification of conservatism and libertarianism can be seen in Ancient Israel. If indeed God is the author of liberty, we would expect the nation he established to be a stateless association of kinsmen with no legislature, no executive, no standing army, and no police; a nation in which, with no state regulating his business, construction, or personal life, "every man did what was right in his own eyes," constrained only by the right of any other man to appeal to a judge for the resolution of disputes.[98]

When I talk to people about the state of the nation, I find that many of them express sentiments that are reflected in the libertarian position, but when it comes to the voting booth the libertarians have a much smaller representation. It would be an oversimplification to say that abortion is the only issue that keeps conservatives from adopting libertarian principles. They are stuck on their own favorite statist issues: militarism and police-statism immediately come to mind. But conservative American voters are less statist than supposedly conservative politicians, and if it weren't for abortion, the

---

97 Id.

98 For a more detailed discussion of the Biblical basis for a libertarian philosophy, see Appendix B.

typical conservative voter, with his ad hoc checklist of liberties, would by now have adopted a more consistent system of principled liberty.

If it weren't for their critical mistake on the issue of abortion, I'm nearly certain that libertarians would dominate the political landscape. By now they would have assimilated the popular conservatives, and even some of the intellectual class of neo-conservatives. In just a handful of election cycles the federal government would have been reduced to a relatively insignificant annoyance–a minor parasite charged with the national defense and little else. Liberty would be on the rise, and prosperity would abound.

Libertarianism's pure, radical ideology on freedom has attracted some, but its position on abortion has turned away the bulk of American conservatives. It has remained the home of a small, powerful intellectual elite on the one hand, and a small band of anti-war protesters, drug users, and sexual deviants on the other. This is particularly unfortunate, because America was founded by classical liberals on the principles of liberty that are now found only in the libertarian camp, and they still hold the key to restoring freedom in our country. Because of their tragically erroneous stance on abortion, the libertarians will never have the political means to restore our liberties, for conservatives will never join them.

If liberty means having to accept the slaughter of innocent unborn babies, the conservative would rather live with an inconsistent, *ad hoc* list of freedoms won or lost in every election cycle. If pure liberty means a right to abortion and the only alternative is a perpetual struggle in which the winner forces his ideology down everyone else's throat, they'd rather fight.

Fortunately, we no longer have to make that choice. A correct analysis of the libertarian ethic does not support a right to an abortion any more than it does a right to murder. *We don't have to recognize abortion rights in order to make a commitment to principled liberty.* The conservative need not join the Libertarian Party; he can simply embrace a consistent ethic of liberty.

The Property-Rights Basis for Libertarian Ethics

Just as there are natural laws of physics, such as the law of gravitation and the first law of motion, so also is there a natural law of law, that is, a natural ethic built into the fabric of the universe by its creator. It's modern form was developed by Murray N. Rothbard, the founder of the libertarian movement and student of Austrian economist Ludwig Von Mises.

Rothbard showed that this natural law is based on the principle of "original appropriation;" if you are the first to put something to use, you are its original owner.[99] You are the only one who has just title to it. The only way for anyone else to obtain just title to it is to get if from you in a voluntary transaction; you can give it to him, trade it, or sell it. Any other means of acquiring title is unjust and must be forbidden. Further, from this first principle there follows a universal set of ethics that determines "justice" between people in all their interactions.

The practical consequence of this universal natural law is that the only just ethical system is one that protects property rights. That is, the protection of property rights is the foundation of all justice in legal, civil, economic, and political systems. This is not to say that property rights is the most important consideration in your life, but only that

---

99 See Appendix A for a discussion of the proof of this universal law of ethics.

it is the only just consideration in determining your rights vis-á-vis other people. That is, there are certain things you *should* or *should not* do, but which you may not be *forbidden* or *required* to do. Maybe you shouldn't watch six hours of television every day instead of playing catch with your ten-year-old, but no state should forbid you to. It might be noble, charitable, and commendable for you to give some of your money to a hungry man, but it is unjust for someone else – like the government – to steal it from you and give it to him, because you own your money and have the sole right to determine what to do with it.

Similarly, the principle of original appropriation applies to ownership of your body. You are the original and sole owner of your own body, and any aggression against it violates your property rights. If you pull a drowning man out of the water, you've done a good thing, but the government can't force you to do so, or punish you for failing to, because this would be enslavement.[100]

Rothbard's Body-Ownership Non Sequitur

So far so good, but this is where Rothbard went wrong on the issue of abortion:

> *The proper groundwork for analysis of abortion is in every man's absolute right of self-ownership. This implies immediately that every woman has the absolute right to her own body, and that she has absolute dominion over her body and everything within it. This includes the fetus.*[101]

---

100 Again, this only addresses your rights, not your moral obligations. Even in an ideal libertarian society, your refusal to save a drowning man would have undesirable consequences. You'd be reviled and discriminated against, or shunned. The government wouldn't be permitted to punish you, but your friends, family, and acquaintances might well refuse to have any further dealings with you.

101 Murray N. Rothbard, *The Ethics of Liberty* (New York: New York University Press, 2002), 98.

Every analysis of rights begins with the property rights involved. In this case we're talking about the right of the mother to have an abortion, and Rothbard is correct to begin with her right of self-ownership and conclude that she has absolute dominion over her body. His mistake is in jumping to the conclusion that she has absolute dominion over *"everything within it."*

That can't possibly be true; let's just take a look at some of the absurd consequences of this doctrine.

Suppose XYZ Corporation has a secret production process stored on a microchip. It's the only copy of the manufacturing instructions for an amazing new widget. They store it in a vault and seek investors to finance its production. When they go back to the vault, they find the chip missing and can't go into production. It was her, Rothbard's lady; she stole a microchip full of industrial secrets from XYZ Corporation and surgically implanted it in her thigh to hide it. By Rothbard's logic, with her absolute dominion over her body and everything in it, the company has no recourse. They can't surgically remove the chip against her will, and they can't even sequester her, because to do so would be to interfere with her absolute dominion over everything within her body. She disappears. A few months later, ABC Corporation in Singapore begins distributing XYZ's widget.

In fact, if she has absolute dominion over everything within her body, if her ownership of what's in her body is actually *absolute*, that would mean that XYZ has no title whatsoever to anything within her body, *not even a right of future possession of the chip once it came back out of her body*. It would mean that she could acquire clear title to stolen property by placing it temporarily within her body, perhaps by swallowing it. You'd have an entire industry of people who specialized in placing valuable objects within bodily orifices momentarily in order to acquire clear title. I could walk into a jewelry store and stuff my mouth full of diamonds, and then sell them with impunity five minutes later.

Let's take the logic a step further. Why would you have to place the object inside a bodily orifice? Could you just completely surround the object with your flesh, as by enclosing it within your hand? What's magical about the moist interior of the mouth? My hand is just as much mine as my mouth is. And if my closed fist is not "within" my body, then neither is my closed mouth or, for that matter, my digestive tract, which is simply a passageway through my body and open at both ends. And if that's not within my body, then neither is the womb "within" the mother's body, as it also is open to the outside.

The logical extension of this whole line of reasoning is that I could simply place my hand around a diamond and *voila*, it's mine. But let's concede for a moment that an object in my fist is not within my body, whereas if I swallow it, it is; for this is no doubt how we commonly understand the term "within." It still begs the question, what is special about being *within* the body? Why would someone acquire one set of property rights to an object within the body, but another set of property rights to an object that is merely grasped in the hand? Rothbard does not explain how "within-ness" affects title differently than mere possession, and it's not obvious to me. Either way, even if going within the body confers some new sort of title to the object, the degree or quality of title thus acquired certainly cannot be absolute, because that would violate the property rights of the true owner. The mere fact that a fetus is present within the mother's body is not sufficient to give her absolute dominion or title to it, which means that it is possible for someone else to have some degree of title to it, some property right over it. That could be the fetus itself, or it could be the one who contributed the genetic material that was in part responsible for its existence – the father.

It may also be argued that because the fetus originated within the mother's body, she is therefore the original appropriator of the fetus, and that as a result there is no other owner whose property rights are violated, but this misconstrues the principle of original appropriation. Original appropriation occurs when a man finds an existing resource in a state of nature and makes use of it for the first time. When Robinson Crusoe cuts down saplings to create a shelter, those saplings become his, and no one else can acquire just title to them except through a voluntary transaction with him.[102]

But one does not simply *find* an existing fetus in a state of nature and lay claim to it; it is *created* by the joint act of two persons. The mother cannot conceive a child alone. If it applies at all, the principle of original appropriation would give joint title to both the mother and the father. The situation is akin to a case of joint title, as when two people share in the expense of an indivisible good, like a house. If the mother's role as originator gives her title to the fetus, then the father has an equal property right as co-originator.

Furthermore, normal family dynamics testify to an implicit acknowledgment of a joint interest in the unborn child after conception. Yes, the mother's body nurtures the fetus, but the father is himself busy providing for the mother and the fetus. It's a cooperative effort, not only when the fetus

---

102 There is a special case for abandonment. If Crusoe abandons the shelter, it becomes unowned. If someone else finds it, he may put it to use and thus acquires complete title by a new appropriation. Later we'll discuss the consequences of a father's abandoning his property rights, if any, to the fetus.

is originated, but also during its development in the womb. So if the mother's relationship to the fetus as nurturer gives her a property right to it, then the father has at least some property right of the same quality and for the same reason, because he is very much involved (though indirectly) in the nurture of the fetus. We cannot ignore the fact that fathers – at least in normally-functioning families – feel an emotional, even a physical, attachment to their unborn children. Of course, this is not proof of title, but it certainly indicates a perception on the father's part that he has some rights with respect to the unborn child.

I have not fully worked out the scope of the property interests and rights involved here. The fetus' property right in himself might only be potential and not mature until he is capable of exercising it, which would be some number of years after his birth. In this case, his self-ownership might be held in trust by the parents.

If so, this trust relationship, which continues until a child is able to provide for himself, is also the basis of the solution to another difficult ethical problem proposed by Rothbard – his assertion of a parent's legal right to allow a child to die for lack of nurture, e.g., by failing to feed him.[103] He demonstrates quite convincingly that imposing a legal obligation on the parents to keep the child alive has tyrannical implications, but the idea that the parent has a right to allow the child to die is itself hideous.

The parental trustee-ownership of the child might be the solution. In the broadest terms, the trustee-ownership of the child obligates the holder of this form of title to provide certain things for the child including, for example, food. The trust title is held by the parents unless they abandon it, which

---

103 Rothbard, *The Ethics of Liberty*, 100.

they can do at any time. The parent-child relationship is not a contract – to enforce specific performance on the parents would be tantamount to enslavement.

If they do abandon the trustee-ownership of the child, a third person may take it and become the child's trustee, and so prevent his death; but if he does, then he assumes all aspects of the title and cannot demand any performance or compensation from the parents. The parental trust title would not require or even justify state intervention, but would only allow an intervening third person to raise an affirmative defense against a charge of kidnapping, for example, by demonstrating that he interfered with the parents' custody of the child only because they abandoned their responsibilities attached to the title as trustees. This would be similar to a "defense of a third-person" affirmative defense to a charge of assault or murder.

What about the case in which no one discovers that the parents have abandoned their trusteeship of the child, or the parents have attempted to find someone else to take the trusteeship, but failed? Consider the parents of a severely handicapped child who requires expensive, constant care. They search, but cannot find anyone willing to take the child. They beg, but no one is willing to assist them financially or in any other way. Given the choice between abject poverty for the whole family or just letting the child die, they let him die.

In a free society, with the great prosperity that naturally flows from liberty, this case would be exceedingly rare, more in the realm of theory than reality. Even today in our country, with our stifling tax burden, it is hard to imagine that these parents couldn't find a charity somewhere to provide some assistance. In a prosperous free country, it is almost inconceivable. But even if it did sometimes occur, creating a state-interventionist mechanism to enforce legal parental obligations is a solution vastly worse than the problem.[104]

The "Coercive Invasive Parasite" Error

Rothbard's next error is in his analysis of the fetus as a parasitic "invader:"

> *Most fetuses are in the mother's womb because the mother consents to this situation, but the fetus is there by the mother's freely-granted consent. But should the mother decide that she does not want the fetus there any longer, then the fetus becomes a parasitic "invader" of her person, and the mother has the perfect right to expel this invader from her domain. Abortion should be looked upon, not as "murder" of a living person, but as the expulsion of an unwanted invader from the mother's body. Any laws restricting or prohibiting abortion are therefore invasions of the rights of mothers....*
>
> *[L]et us concede, for purposes of this discussion, that fetuses are human beings – or, more broadly, potential human beings – and are therefore entitled to full human rights. But what humans, we may ask, have the right to be coercive parasites within the body of an unwilling human host? Clearly, no born humans have such a right, and therefore, a fortiori, the fetus can have no such right either.[105]*

---

104 A collateral benefit of eliminating all state involvement in the care and upbringing of the child is that it places a greater value on family and community relationships. To the extent that parents can rely on the state to take over in cases of difficulty with the children, they have less need for the help of family and friends. If, on the other hand, they can't fall back on the state, then family, friends, neighbors, and charities become more valuable. Relationships in general become more valuable, and in order to "purchase" more and better relationships, the parents make themselves more attractive to others. This encourages civility, nobility, generosity, hospitality – in fact, all the indicators of good neighborliness.

105 Id. at 98.

The first error in this analysis is in attributing to the fetus the status of an "invader." To "invade" is to enter as an enemy with a view to conquest or plunder; to infringe, encroach upon, or violate; to penetrate; or to permeate. To speak of the fetus as an invader makes no sense. Of course, he cannot willingly move into or out of the womb, but even calling him an invader in the metaphorical sense implies that he has done something to change his relation in some way vis-à-vis the mother. But this is not the case at all. He did nothing to get himself there, and when the mother later decides not to have a baby after all, his sudden status as an "invader" is entirely due to her whim. Now she has an absolute right to discard this invader by killing him?

If you're going to concede for this argument that the fetus is alive – and Rothbard does – you can't just pass a death sentence on him without addressing his innocence or culpability. If the libertarian ethic has any concern for justice, we can't say that the absence of a volitional act on his part is irrelevant. The fetus has not done anything to acquire the status of an invader. It was entirely due to the mother's whim. How can a death sentence be just, in this case?

Suppose the mother in Rothbard's example was a ship's captain. Our captain sails past a tropical island a thousand miles from the nearest land, and sees a shipwrecked crew waving frantically for her attention. She brings them aboard her ship and sets sail for their home. Halfway there, still 500 miles from land, on a whim she withdraws her consent for their presence aboard her ship. It's her ship, her property, and they are now invaders not because of anything they did, but because of her whim. They refuse to jump overboard, so she tosses them, and after several exhausting hours they drown. Has she not committed murder? If she hasn't, then what would be the difference if she brought them aboard with the intent to throw them overboard a few days later? Certainly they came aboard with her consent, and as soon as she decided to throw them overboard her consent ceased, but up to that point they were there by her consent. Yet all along she intended them to die, and her action, not theirs, is what caused their death.

Contrast that situation with the case in which the rescuees stage a mutiny. The saved shipwrecked crew rebels against the authority of the captain, seeks to depose her, and perhaps to kill her. Now she is justified in withdrawing her consent for their presence on her ship, and the consequence of their banishment is on their own heads. But the reason for the different result – the reason a death sentence is just in one case but not the other – is tied to the volitional act on the part of the rescuees.

The second error here lies in Rothbard's asserted equivalency between the fetus as a parasite and a born human as a parasite. That is, Rothbard compares born-human parasitism and fetal parasitism, assumes that they have the same qualities, and then concludes that since a born human has no right to be a parasite, neither does a fetus.

I don't deny that the fetus' existence is parasitic in that he cannot survive apart from the energy and nurture provided by the mother's body. The error is in the assertion of equivalency. It is not in the nature of a born human to be a parasite within the body of another human host. The very idea is rather grotesque. It would undeniably be an aggression of one's right of self-ownership to force him to host a born-human parasite.

But it manifestly is in the nature of a fetus to be a parasite in the body of the mother until his birth. In a born human, parasitism is unnatural and grotesque, and in the case in which someone is being deliberately parasitic, it is morally reprehensible. But in the case of a fetus, parasitism is the natural order of creation. A normal born human is able to provide for himself, and the only consequence of forbidding him to parasitize another person is that he will be denied a life of parasitic leisure. But when you forbid a fetus to parasitize, you sentence him to death. To hold the fetus to the same standard as a born human being on the issue of his parasitism is nonsensical, sort of like expecting the fetus to get a job and provide for himself.

The third error in Rothbard's parasitism analysis is in his discussion of the fact that the mother is being coerced. If the host is willing, there is no issue; the mother bears the fetus to term and the child is born. But if she is not willing, the argument goes, forcing her to bear the child to term is an aggression against her right of self-ownership; in other words, the pregnancy is forced labor, or enslavement.

But the question is not whether she's being coerced, but why. Yes, we're coercing her to bear the child, but the reason is that if we allow her to do what she wants, it will kill the fetus. All we're doing is restraining her from committing murder. It's an imposition similar in kind to restraining the ship captain from tossing her passengers overboard to drown, although it is concededly more of an imposition in *quantity*, because she will suffer this restraint until the child is born.

This imposition is indistinguishable from self-defense, or more accurately, defense of a third person. If a thug lifts an axe over his head to chop you down, you can use force to restrain him from harming you; and if I was there, I could do it to protect you even if I had no other interest in either of you. That's precisely what's going on when the mother is coerced into bearing the child instead of killing him.

Dealing With the Difficult Cases

We have demonstrated that the property-rights basis of a libertarian ethic does not give a woman an absolute right to have an abortion. So far we have addressed the case in which the mother initially wanted to get pregnant, but then changes her mind, and we've shown that she cannot simply discard the fetus. Now let's examine some of the consequences of this reasoning in various other circumstances.

The mother accidentally gets pregnant. Here the mother simply assumes the risk of her sexual activity. The unborn child is not culpable.

The mother and father agree not to have the baby. If the mother and the father were the only ones with a property right to the unborn child, then they could not be compelled to bear him to term. But there is one other involved in the equation; the unborn child himself, and so we need to examine his self-ownership in more detail.

Rothbard himself showed that one human cannot justly completely own another, and that even in the case of a fetus, the mother does not own him in "fee simple";[106] otherwise, he would be born her slave and remain so even into his adulthood. The parent only owns the "parental rights" to the child, whatever those may be.[107] That leaves the child with some remaining rights, but as he is in the womb he is incapable of exercising them. Until he is capable of doing so, the parents hold his rights in trust for his benefit. One of those rights is the same that all other humans have, the right

---

106 "Fee simple" means complete title, total ownership of all possible property rights.

107 It is not necessary for this discussion to delineate those rights. For Rothbard's discussion on this point, see Rothbard, *The Ethics of Liberty*, especially ch. 14: Children and Rights, pp. 97-112.

to defend oneself against unjust harm.[108] Thus, the parents must defend him from unjust killing and certainly cannot kill him themselves.

The mother is raped. Once again, the child has done nothing here to merit a death sentence. The mother certainly has been violated and is, against her will, going to bear the burden of pregnancy and then of upbringing, but her recourse is against the rapist, not the innocent unborn child.

The child is the product of incest. Though incest might well be morally deviant sexual behavior, the culprits here are the parents, not the child, and he still must be protected from murder.

The mother will die unless she aborts the baby. Frankly, I don't know how to handle this situation. True, the baby is still not culpable, but what about the mother? Is her culpability relevant? Does it matter if the pregnancy resulted from illicit sexual behavior? Or if she was raped? What if she and her husband wanted the baby, but learned the pregnancy would kill the mother? Can she not treat herself against this lethal condition? Does it matter whether the baby was also likely to die, in which case it's simply a matter of accelerating the inevitable for him in order to prevent her death?

One thing to keep in mind is that in an ideal libertarian society, in a truly free country, there would be no state to make this decision based on political considerations. There would be no prosecutor with political ambitions to bring charges against the mother. There would only be interested family

---

108 Rothbard argues that under libertarian law, "capital punishment would have to be confined strictly to the crime of murder." Id. at 85. Without agreeing or disagreeing with this point, it is sufficient to point out that the unborn child is not capable of murder or any other crime.

members, friends, neighbors, or, at worst, nosy busybodies in the community who might press charges. There would be tremendous prudential considerations (as opposed to political ones) involved in deciding whether to press charges; family members would sympathize with the parents and would almost certainly have advised them already, in which case they probably would not bring charges. The same is true for friends, neighbors, and fellow church-members. In the worst case, an obnoxious busybody might cause problems, but a free society would have a lot of leeway to "punish" that kind of behavior by exclusion, discrimination, and in fact, peer pressure of every kind. Without condoning it, I would just point out that it wouldn't be unheard-of for such an obnoxious member of the community to suffer a "blanket party,[109]" or maybe just a secretive, late-night, very stern warning to mind his own business, to leave things alone or else.[110]

Another consideration is just how very different court cases would be in a free society. Our jurisprudence is in the sorry condition it's in precisely because the state has replaced natural law jurisprudence with political law jurisprudence; judges are now mere interpreters of incomprehensible and

---

109 A blanket party is a means of corporal punishment conducted by a peer group, such as the military. The victim is covered with a blanket and struck repeatedly.

110 This obnoxious person might be a member of a very activist and fanatical pro-life group, but I mention this only to make the point that a truly free society would, in this way, minimize the impact of the societal fringe groups. Environmentalist nuts, animal rights thugs, militant pro-choicers, homeless bums, and homosexual rights activists would not be rewarded for their anti-social positions, as they are in a democratic society like ours, which provides a political "gravy train" for every variety of social deviancy. The democratic process stimulates social dysfunction and deviancy and is in this way decivilizing, whereas a free society naturally stimulates socially functional norms, and is in this way civilizing. Indeed, to get your way in a democratic society, you have to march, vandalize, make noise, and get in people's faces. The more obnoxious and repulsive you are, the more money and privilege you get from the state; you don't win people to your cause, you just find a politician who will trade some of his power, privilege, and money in exchange for your vote. To get your way in a free society, you have to be noble, persuasive, and in every way attractive, in order to win people to your cause voluntarily.

self-contradictory legislation. They have lost the skill to resolve difficult ethical problems, but in a free society they would quickly relearn these lost principles of justice and would soon be dispensing wise rulings.

In any event, it makes no sense to try to extract universal principles from the rarest, most difficult cases. On the contrary, fundamental principles are clear from the fundamental cases and then applied by brighter minds in the more difficult ones. So it would be unwise to use this very difficult circumstance as the basis for a general rule regarding the ethics of abortion.

26

LIBERTY AND THE TEA PARTY AGENDA

If the Tea Party is the best hope for restoring liberty in America, we need to be sure our mission and agenda are founded in liberty-oriented principles. Our stated mission is in three parts; fiscal responsibility, limited government, and free markets. Let's examine these.

———⊗⊗⊗———

Fiscal Responsibility. We're going to have to face the fact we can't expect fiscal responsibility out of Washington, and plan accordingly. Fundamental principles of economics dictate that it's impossible. In a democracy, or a democratic republic, or a parliamentary commonwealth, or any government with a democratic apparatus, the capital value of the nation is publicly owned. The elected official is a temporary caretaker who doesn't own the capital value of the nation, but only the benefit of its present use, i.e., whatever value he's able to extract from it right now. Since he doesn't own the capital value he can't profit from it, so he has no economic incentive to preserve it. On the contrary, his only incentive is to consume as much of it as possible to purchase the votes he needs to remain in office. He doesn't care if what he does now will bankrupt the country in the future. Fiscal irresponsibility is a characteristic of the governmental system. The very existence of the Social Security program proves this beyond dispute.

The Tea Party's strategy is to elect candidates who are committed to being fiscally responsible, which is certainly laudable. Occasionally a candidate brings strong personal convictions to his office and tries to be sensible. With a great deal of vigilance, it might be possible, during a few election cycles, to keep the pressure on the candidate and obtain some temporary reduction in spending, taxation, and debt, but in the long term, corrupted as he is just by being in the government apparatus, he can't resist. He will either succumb to the irresistible, corruptive influences or return home. Either way, spending, taxes, and deficits will resume their relentless upward trend.

Even to the extent that we succeed in bringing some fiscal responsibility to Washington, we have not clearly defined an amount of spending, taxation, and debt that we call "fiscally responsible." The reason, of course, is that the only logically consistent position is too radical for mass consumption; any amount of taxation is irresponsible, for there's no way to characterize the systematic institutionalized theft of someone's money as responsible. Even if you say "we need roads," and overlook the fact that private road systems are doable and better, you can't justify theft just because you need roads. In just a moment we'll discuss the Tea Party's call for free markets, but for now note that you wouldn't need public roads if you allowed a free market for roads. Public roads are simply a subsidy that distorts the free market for roads, leading to excesses at some times, shortages at others, and waste in every case.

This is not to say that we should reject the chance to have some amount of fiscal responsibility. Given the choice between a needle in the eye or one in the foot, I'll take one in the foot. There are degrees of irresponsibility, and less irresponsibility is better than more. More debt, spending, and taxation is more irresponsible than less of them. Also, some *kinds* of taxation are more reprehensible than others; taxing only some people, or some people more than others, is more reprehensible than taxes that apply to everyone. Income taxes, estate taxes, and any other kind of wealth-based taxes are more reprehensible than consumption taxes, use taxes, or other taxes of general and equal applicability.

So yes, let's demand fiscal responsibility. But we have to keep in mind that the only surefire way to eliminate government waste is to cut off its money. When you drive a thousand miles for a vacation at the ocean, it makes no sense to stop a block away from the beach.

Limited Government. Certainly, limited government is better than unlimited government, but limited government inexorably grows beyond its limitations no matter what a Constitution says. Governments have a monopoly of taxation, and government agents are net tax-consumers. Assuming nothing more than their self-interest, government agents will always increase their exploitation of taxpayers, and the government will grow. Even if there were some way to confine the government to a single constitutional role, it would forever increase the quantity of whatever single service it provided, and it would end up as the same immense regulatory regime we suffer today.[111] The historical evidence

---

111 See ch. 6: *Can We Limit Government?*

is clear; our own government today is manifestly not the limited government our founders established.

Restoring some liberties is great, but establishing complete liberty is the final victory, and should be our default goal. We may not soon abolish government entirely, but we must at least understand that even if somehow we succeeded in restoring our liberties all the way to the full extent of the liberties enjoyed by our founders, and even improved them, later generations will repeat this struggle. Why condemn them to the same oppression we're fighting now?

Sure, join the fight for limited government over the present totalitarian regime, but as we approach the goal, set your sights yet higher. The government the founders established has failed to live out the course they charted for it. With the benefit of hindsight and the work of people like Murray Rothbard, Hans-Hermann Hoppe, and other Austrian Economists, we now have a more complete understanding of what it takes to secure liberty. This time we could actually hope to secure our liberties permanently by avoiding the errors of the past in attempting the impossible task of establishing a constitutionally limited government.

Free Markets. The Tea Party's demand for free markets is consistent with liberty. But does it really demand free markets across the board? My personal experience is that tea partiers do not demand a free market for marijuana, for example. If the government has the constitutional power to regulate products in the market, which products it regulates is just a matter of who won the last election, and the markets are not safe.

I mention this only because it's a sticking point for tea partiers on the issue of free markets. They don't know how to respond to the charge that they're inconsistent in demanding free markets while wanting to regulate drugs.

As Jefferson said, "I would rather be exposed to the inconveniences attending too much liberty than to those attending too small a degree of it." A principled, liberty-oriented stance on free markets indeed demands that people have the right to use drugs if they wish. Our consolation, at least, is that the social situation would be better than it is under the intensive regulation of the War on Drugs. In a truly free country that didn't reward non-productivity with welfare benefits, drug use would sharply decline as people became more far-sighted, more responsible for their own welfare, their income, their savings, and their retirement. In an unregulated economy, drug users automatically pay for their stupidity and are quickly marginalized.

Admittedly, drug use increases the tendency for people to commit crimes, but controlling the factors of crime instead of the crime itself infringes on everyone's liberties. A sugar rush makes my neighbor more irritable and increases his tendency to be violent, but regulating how much sugar people ingest infringes my liberty to eat however much sugar I want. I don't abuse sugar; why should the government punish me because my neighbor does? It's exactly the same kind of regulation as the regulation of marijuana, and whether it gets regulated is just a question of who gets elected. Alcohol is the case in chief; if social utility were what mattered, it should be banned. I guess politicians have their pet vices.

The only way to keep the government from regulating your business is to forbid it to regulate *anything* in the market. A free market means no regulations or subsidies of any kind, not even welfare in any of its forms. Instead of subsidizing drug addicts, a free country with a free market would let them fail. True liberty demands that we let truly, completely free markets handle the drug user. His productivity will suffer and he will, at best, wind up in the hands of a charity that actually holds him accountable, unlike government welfare programs.

The Tea Party is reliably conservative, but we have just seen that strictly consistent principles of unfettered liberty are found only in the libertarian position, and so to win our liberties one of two things must occur; either the Tea Party must join the Libertarian Party instead of the Republican Party, or else libertarianism must become the basis of Tea Party thinking.

The first possibility – joining the Libertarian Party – would have the benefit of adopting a structure that is already built on fully developed libertarian principles. That is, the libertarians already know and understand the principles of liberty; the Republicans don't. However, this strategy poses some great challenges. For one thing, the Republican Party is already in place, whereas taking the Libertarian Party to the status of majority party would mean displacing the entire Republican Party apparatus and erecting a new party in its place in Washington, instead of just slipping into an ongoing operation.[112]

Another problem with joining the Libertarian Party is that we'd be switching horses in the middle of the race. A tremendous amount of resources are already committed to the current strategy, and switching now would put us behind by at least one election cycle and more likely several. Retooling would give the opposition – which consists of

---

112 Of course, the systemically dysfunctional apparatus of the Republican Party will itself be a mighty impediment, if the Tea Party is successful in taking it over. They are entrenched in the Washington power structure, and tea party newbies are going to be told "you don't know how things are done around here." Their response needs to be, "we're not doing things that way anymore."

both the left and the ruling-class right – an opportunity to mount a counter attack, and we could lose the current advantage of momentum.

Finally, moving tea partiers to the Libertarian Party is psychologically a lot more demanding than gradually educating them as to their natural liberty-oriented affinity with libertarian ideology and having it bloom within the ranks of the Republican Party. For a tea partier to take the affirmative step of abandoning the Republican Party would require him to consciously, positively prefer the Libertarian Party despite its official position on abortion.

The other alternative – cultivating libertarian ideology within the Tea Party wing of the Republican Party – requires only that tea partiers learn and embrace libertarianism within the context of activities they're already committed to. Until now even this has been impossible because of the issue of abortion, for Rothbard's influential variety of libertarianism upholds a woman's absolute right to an abortion, and this view is reflected in the official platform of the Libertarian Party. The tea partiers represent the heartland of American politics, and abortion is an emotional, hot-button issue closely associated with their ideological enemy, the liberal left. While tea partiers would otherwise have a great affinity with libertarianism, abortion alone has been enough to make them reject the entire libertarian ideology. I speak from personal experience.[113]

But I say it has been a problem only *until now* because a correct analysis of the property-rights basis of the libertarian

---

113 The Tea Party's public thrust is primarily fiscal, but this is a tactic to avoid an internal rift on the issue of abortion. The strategy is "fiscal responsibility, free markets, and limited government," and the tactic is to avoid the social issues. But the reality is that a very large bloc of tea partiers, likely a majority, are pro-life, and the next-largest group is pro-choice due to a mistaken belief that a consistent liberty-oriented ethic requires it. Many of them will actually be relieved to learn of their mistake.

ethic *does not* support a right to have an abortion. Tea partiers can now feel free to study and embrace libertarianism and understand that it is the founding principle of our nation, and today it is the only ideology which can restore our liberties to their original state, and even better.

Joining the Libertarian Party is one thing, but learning and embracing libertarian ideals is another thing entirely. As long as the Libertarian Party still holds its position on abortion, there's no chance we'll join, but it's totally reasonable for us to embrace the other liberty-oriented principles of modern libertarianism. Abortion has been the major obstacle to reconciling the tea party and libertarian ideology, but now that Rothbard's analysis is clearly seen to be in error, all we need to do is get the word out to the tea partiers everywhere that libertarian thinking will get us more liberty than any other ideology.

Of course, there remain some challenges. Libertarianism's call for the abolition of the state is too much for a lot of people. They're not prepared to deal with incredulous questions from friends and family – and of course opponents – like "oh yeah? Well who's gonna pay for roads, huh?" The founders seriously considered these issues, and it was a close call as to whether even to have a federal government, but today we're so far down the road to totalitarianism that even those hungry for liberty have a hard time even accurately imagining it. Picture John Boehner answering media questions about a proposal to flat-out eliminate social security, and it gives you some idea of the scope of the problem. He can't even fight like a girl for four days' worth of spending cuts; he's not going to fight for something really significant like *liberty*.

We can't expect politicians to lead on these issues. It's much easier to *follow*; elected officials float positions and see which ones attract a mass of voters. If they lead, they run the risk of losing. So as far as leadership, that's up to us; but then, that's what the Tea Party is all about.

The entire Tea Party movement is grassroots, which means action from the bottom up, voters pushing a candidate for office with specific instructions about what to do when they get to Washington. This will achieve some restoration of liberties, and so it's a cause worthy of our effort. But the danger always remains that even our starry-eyed candidates will become either assimilated or disillusioned. If assimilated, it's a turn to the Dark Side and they become statist. If disillusioned, they come back home, and only the statists remain in Washington.

We must hold the politicians strictly liable when they fail to carry out the mandate to fight for and restore our liberties. That's why we must remain constantly vigilant; why we must demand nothing but complete liberty; why we must continue to learn – and teach – the principles of liberty we're fighting for.

Even within the Tea Party we must expect varying degrees of commitment to principles of liberty. Some will be satisfied with slowing down the spending a little, and maybe a moderate reduction in the income tax. Some will demand more, perhaps a balanced budget amendment. Only a few will be purists when it comes to liberty, but those are the only ones who can anchor the movement to a consistent, principled foundation.

Even while we use the current top-down political strategy to restore our freedoms (by using the government apparatus to try to reduce the power of government), we must also continue the work at the grassroots level itself. It's only here that we can be sure of the results.

We need a change of mind; think of yourselves as free men in a police state. How should you live? By keeping in mind that liberty is the gift of God and should not be scorned. We have to find ways to exercise and extend our liberties. Wherever and whenever it's possible to circumvent government intervention, we should do so. So long as it's legal to buy a gun in a private sale, and so avoid the background check, we should do so. So long as we can legally join a herd-share co-op and buy raw milk, we should do so.

Those are small examples, but there are momentous ones too. It might take a decade of work to improve the public school system by half, but you can educate your kids yourself, or send them to a private school. It might take national bankruptcy for the government to kick your drug-addicted relative off the welfare rolls, but you can stop enabling him right now. National healthcare might be here to stay, God forbid, but there is an exemption for certain qualifying healthcare sharing ministries you could join instead. You can also examine the health benefits of herbal and homeopathic medicine, and of a diet of natural foods. Support local farmers, and use health clinics that don't take Medicare and Medicaid.

You'll recognize these opportunities by the fact that they tend to come up in the context of family, church, and small-community dynamics. One long-term project that could yield tremendous dividends: establish a voluntary judicial system in your family, clan, church, or community. Instead of submitting your disputes to the dysfunctional state judicial system, have the "village elders" resolve them. The scope of jurisdiction could cover anything you all agreed to, including property covenants, contract disputes, nuisances, vandalism, and assault, and you could even have different systems in adjoining communities; in other words, create a free market for judicial production.

All of these ways of exercising liberty are eminently realistic and doable, and yet they are manifestations of a phenomenon that people trapped in a statist mentality are afraid to even think about, much less deliberately execute it. What we're talking about here is the phenomenon of systemic – as opposed to territorial – secession.

People everywhere always have a natural right of secession. The United States was founded on an act of secession. You may have read the Declaration of Independence before, but read it again now with a focus on what Jefferson said about breaking away from unjust rule:

———— ∞ ————

When in the Course of human events it becomes necessary for one people to dissolve the political bands which have connected them with another and to assume among the powers of the earth, the separate and equal station to which the Laws of Nature and of Nature's God entitle them, a decent respect to the opinions of mankind requires that they should declare the causes which impel them to the separation.

We hold these truths to be self-evident, that all men are created equal, that they are endowed by their Creator with certain unalienable Rights, that among these are Life, Liberty and the pursuit of Happiness. — That to secure these rights, Governments are instituted among Men, deriving their just powers from the consent of the governed, — That whenever any Form of Government becomes destructive of these ends, it is the Right of the People to alter or to abolish it, and to institute new Government, laying its foundation on such principles and organizing its powers in such form, as to them shall

*seem most likely to effect their Safety and Happiness.
Prudence, indeed, will dictate that Governments long
established should not be changed for light and transient
causes; and accordingly all experience hath shewn that
mankind are more disposed to suffer, while evils are
sufferable than to right themselves by abolishing the
forms to which they are accustomed. But when a long
train of abuses and usurpations, pursuing invariably
the same Object evinces a design to reduce them under
absolute Despotism, it is their right, it is their duty, to
throw off such Government, and to provide new Guards
for their future security.*

The right of secession is self-evident, but that doesn't
guarantee that it will be successful; the Civil War proved that.
This was a territorial secession in the context of the sharply
polarizing ideological issue of human slavery.

But the sort of systemic secession at issue for us is very
different. First, today the ideological issue is in favor of
the would-be secessionists. In the Civil War the issue for
the secessionists was "states rights," but the issue for the
Union was individual liberty. The fact that it was more of a
rallying cry for the Union than a principle to which they were
genuinely dedicated only proves the power of the issue itself
to affect public opinion.

Today the issue of individual liberty is on the side of the
Tea Party. What does the opposition have? Social justice?
Egalitarianism? That might have worked a century ago, but
since then the Berlin Wall has come down, and I doubt that
even then it would have worked here. Dwindling though it
may be, there is too long a tradition of rugged individualism
in America.

The other key difference is the fact that we're not talking about moving all tea partiers to Utah, Texas, or Montana and voting to secede. We're talking about seceding right in place. Think about it. Your neighbors might think you're a little weird for handling your disputes internally, sending your kids to private school, and buying organic produce, but would they be willing to kill you to stop you? And even if the central government decided to crack down, if it happened everywhere, where would they invade?

This kind of thing is unstoppable.

Before long we would have Free Trade Zones. Picture little Monacos, Hong Kongs, and Liechtensteins all over the United States. Not at first, of course, for the federal government would not immediately suspend federal regulations and taxes, but state and local governments could more easily suspend state and local regulations and taxes in counties or parts of them.

Imagine neighborhoods, towns, or even counties in which the State exempted all taxes and regulation – maybe just a few at first, but imagine the suspension of all taxation and regulation. Imagine an experiment in which there were no public services of any kind, where all services were private and competitive. No monopolies. All property was private, even roads. The post offices, the libraries, the schools, the courts, the police departments, the water supplies, and the fire departments, all private, all competitive. No sales tax, property tax, income tax, in fact no taxes or fees of any kind whatsoever, whatever concessions you could obtain from state or local authorities.

The resulting economic boom would attract people and businesses to the area, and soon other communities would be clamoring for similar freedoms. Once a movement like this builds momentum, it is unstoppable – look at the civil rights movement and the fall of the Soviet Union.

So, who can do this? Some are already doing it. At least two million citizens have seceded from government involvement in education, and if we hope to put secessionist principles successfully into practice, we need to study how homeschoolers have done it.

27

HOMESCHOOLING: A MODEL FOR SYSTEMIC SECESSION

Homeschooling is at its core a libertarian (i.e., liberty-oriented) ideology; the rejection of government education. Like any movement in which the participants embrace a complete paradigm shift, it is a radical ideology; the absolute conviction that government education destroys children, and that they must be rescued at any cost. This position brooks no compromise, no attempt by the parents to incrementally improve the school system, for by the time any improvement is seen, it's too late for the children. The government school is seen as hopelessly beyond repair, and parental obligation demands no less than to withdraw the child from the system.

Not everyone who homeschools holds this view, of course. Especially now, a couple of decades after the modern movement began, many are joining the ranks out of a mere pragmatic assessment that it results in a better education. But such people do not start movements or cause great changes in them. Only the radicals do. These are the "roots" of the movement – "radical" is from the Latin for "having roots." These are the ones who homeschooled when it was risky; who organized and supported each other; who created curricula;

who battled in court and in the legislatures; who formed the Home School Legal Defense Association.

Education without the state. That's the radical concept. All we need to do is extend that way of thinking to other civic, social, and cultural activities – which is the foundation of governance. Difficult? Of course, but just like homeschooling, it's worth it. We need to regain a Wild West, Last Frontier, Rugged Individualist, Red-Blooded American can-do outlook regarding freedom. In this day, that's as radical as anything.

Here are some possibilities:

Start a private sports league. Imagine youth baseball without politicians and bureaucrats. It's as simple as starting a league with one overarching rule – no state, local, or municipal government involvement allowed.[114] You would not use any publicly-owned fields or facilities. The people in charge should have experience coaching kids, knowledge of the rules, and a desire to strengthen families through sports. You would no longer have to fight politicians over the purpose of the league. Some private leagues would stress rewarding good players and eliminating bad ones; others would be a home for kids who aren't very good players but still want to have fun.

Be a judge in your family or community. Study and put into practice principles of natural law justice. Discuss your ideas with your immediate family, your extended family, your church, and your community. Offer to resolve disputes as they arise as an alternative to calling the police or suing in the state courts. Encourage wise, experienced members of the community to resolve regular matters such as boundary

---

114 Again, I say "simple," not "easy." The concept is not hard to grasp, although the execution might well involve a lot of effort.

disputes, nuisances like barking dogs or offensive smells, and domestic matters. Learn about resolving disputes between members of a church, and for complex matters consider any number of Christian dispute resolution services.[115] These dispute resolution providers might not be committed to anti-statist principles as such, but just by avoiding state providers you enhance the quality of justice in your particular case.

Find a good family doctor. Healthcare providers are intensely regulated by the state. Find one who understands your concerns and will work with you in such matters as child vaccinations, alternatives to prescription drugs, and home birthing. Some clinics do not accept government-funded patients; this is often a clue that you'll find a cooperative doctor there.

Emphasize Family and Community Self-Reliance. Self-reliance is used in the sense of independence from the state, and reliance on self, family, church, and community. Learn the basics of emergency preparedness and organize an emergency-response team in your neighborhood in cases of storm, flood, fire, or other emergency. Call your neighbors occasionally to see if they need help with anything, thereby fostering a habit of mutual interdependence instead of dependence on the state. For an excellent resource, I recommend an emergency preparedness blog which I maintain at http://www.survivalnewsonline.com.

Bury your own dead. In some states people have the right to bury their own dead on their property with virtually no state interference. If you're so fortunate, exercise those rights

---

115 Icorvi Ministries, official web site, http://www.icorvi.org/index.php; Pedersen Law & Dispute Resolution Corporation, official web site, http://www.pedersenlaw.com/christian_dispute_resolution.html; and the Institute for Christian Conciliation, official web site, http://www.peacemaker.net/site/c.nuIWL7MOJtE/b.5394441/k.BD56/Home.htm, are three of the many resources available.

to keep from losing them. The State of Tennessee is a model of liberty when it comes to burial and funeral laws:[116]

- You don't have to buy a casket from a funeral home. In fact, you don't have to use a casket at all.

- You don't have to claim the body from the funeral home; you can pick up the body yourself at the hospital.

- You don't have to hire a funeral director; you can conduct the funeral service yourself, or have a friend, relative, or total stranger do it, as long as they do it for free. But if they charge a fee for the service, they must be licensed.

- You can bury the deceased on your own property, his property, or a relative's property. By doing so you create a family cemetery. If you want certain tax advantages (and access to the cemetery after you sell the property) you have to register a deed indicating the presence of the family cemetery on the property. Failing to register the cemetery plot only means you can't claim the property tax deduction or access after the property is sold.

Avoid regulated food sources. Join an organic food co-op, buy from local producers, and grow your own. You'll avoid the health hazards of state-cartelized industrial food production.

Use a religious healthcare sharing ministry. Starting in 2014 you'll be fined if you don't buy state-regulated healthcare insurance unless you join an organization like Samaritan Ministries, whose members share healthcare costs. To be sure, a completely free market for health insurance

---

116 Hamilton County Medical Examiner's Office, *Frequently Asked Questions of the Hamilton County Medical Examiner Office*, http://www.hamiltontn.gov/medicalexaminer/me%20office%20faqs.htm (accessed Aug. 16, 2011).

would be much better, but short of paying the fine or joining an Anabaptist church, this is your only alternative.

Because statist policies destroy civilization by destroying the family household, all of these possibilities have a common element – they eliminate *state gateways* into the family and community dynamic. Use your imagination. In what other ways can you divorce yourself, your family, and your community from the state? In every case the goal is *governance without state*, that is, a voluntary association of people, no power to tax, and no monopolies. As much as possible, you would reject the use of public funds, facilities, equipment, or any other public resources. To avoid being infected with a statist way of thinking you might even exclude government employees from whatever program you put into effect.

Our hope for liberty is in your hands. To me, that's encouraging.

APPENDIX A

THE PROPERTY-RIGHTS BASIS OF NATURAL LAW AND THE LIBERTARIAN ETHIC

The libertarian ethic holds that the natural law of justice is based on the principle of original appropriation; that is, that the property right in oneself and in tangible goods is the foundation of natural law. I know of two philosophical proofs in support of this proposition: Rothbard's *argumentum a contrario* and Hoppe's impossibility theorem.

1. Rothbard's *Argumentum a Contrario*[117]

Argumentum a contrario proves its point by eliminating the contrary.

First, the purpose of the argument is to establish a universal human ethic, a rule of justice that applies to all humans as to their humanity.

Second, it is postulated that a man has ownership rights to his own body. If this is true, then we have the universal libertarian ethic: One man may not by the means of aggressive violence impose his will over the natural property rights in the person or tangible goods of another, or else he deprives the other man of his freedom of action with respect to his goods and of the full exercise of his natural self-ownership.

---

117 Rothbard, *The Ethics of Liberty*, 45.

If it is not true, there are two possible conditions: (1) the "communist" universal and equal ownership of others, or (2) partial ownership of one group by another – a system of one class (R) ruling over another class of people (S).

In the second case we have one class of people (R – the rulers) who can own themselves and others (S – the subjects), but members of the group S cannot own themselves entirely, nor any part of the group R. This by definition is not a universal ethic, for it creates two classes of humans, one with superior rights over the other.

In the first case, we do have a universal class with a rule that applies to all equally: No man, A, is entitled to 100% ownership of his own person, considering the rights of all other individuals B, C, D, and so on, and the same holds true for all other individuals with respect to the rights of A. Thus, no man could take any action without everyone else's consent. However, this condition is impossible to perform, and therefore impossible as a universal ethic.

In the first place, if there are more than just a few people in society, it is impossible to communicate with them all, and so getting or giving consent would be impossible. The man intent on having a drink of water would never get consent in time from those in China, or those trapped in a blizzard in Antarctica, or those on a desert expedition far from cell towers or internet; very quickly, the human race would die. In practice, then, the ideal case devolves into the second case (2), partial rule by some over others, as a class forms to "represent" the consent of others, and then once again the ethic collapses for lack of universality.[118] And if the

---

118 The only way out of this quandary would be for all people to register advance consent for all possible contingencies, which would lead to chaos, or to limit advance permission to those circumstances necessary to protect the individual right of 100% self-ownership, which brings us full-circle to the postulated case.

second case is wrong in its absolute application (illustrated by the extreme example of a man dying of thirst for lack of permission to drink) then any steps toward the search of a universal human ethic in that direction are steps in the wrong direction. So a system in which anyone is denied the exercise of self-ownership rights for any reason, to any extent other than to maintain an equal station with other men with respect to their universal ethic (i.e., to prevent encroachment by another), creates a ruling-class system and is itself a system that fails to satisfy the universality requirement.

This leaves 100% self-ownership as the only possible basis for a universal ethic.

2. Hoppe's Impossibility Theorem[119]

Before stating the impossibility theorem it is established

(1) that the purpose of ethics is to resolve conflicts with respect to the proper use of scarce means or economic goods, that is, ethics is concerned with the assignment of control over scarce goods, i.e. *property rights*, in order to rule out conflict; and

(2) that in order to pose an ethical problem, both parties to a conflict must be capable of propositional exchange, i.e. *argumentation*. A flood (or a mosquito) might pose a conflict with respect to the appropriation of a piece of real estate, but the conflict is merely technical, not ethical, unless and until the opponent is capable of pleading his case in the form of a rational argument.

Now let us take Hoppe's proof in his own words:

No one can deny, without falling into performative contradictions, that the common rationality as displayed by the ability to engage in propositional exchange

---

119 Hoppe, *Democracy: The God That Failed*, 201, footnote.

constitutes a necessary condition for ethical problems because this denial would itself have to be presented in the form of a proposition.

Suppose A wanted to claim a piece of jungle land occupied by a disease-bearing mosquito, and B says to A, "the mosquito's ability to engage in propositional exchange is not a necessary condition to raise an ethical conflict with regard to the mosquito's right over this piece of jungle land." Now the ethical issue to be resolved is B's assertion of mosquito property rights, and this puts him squarely in conflict with A. By stating as a proposition (for there's no other way to do it) that propositional exchange is not a precondition for an ethical conflict over a scarce good, B has established *himself* as a party to the conflict. The mosquito, unable to state the proposition one way or the other, remains oblivious. This is what is meant by a performative contradiction. It is, as Professor Hoppe goes on the explain, the *a priori* of argumentation.

Next, he states that this same kind of performative contradiction results whenever *anything* presupposed by argumentation is argumentatively disputed:

> *Second, it is pointed out that everything that must be presupposed by argumentation cannot in turn be argumentatively disputed without getting entangled in a performative contradiction, and that among such presuppositions there exist not only logical ones, such as the laws of propositional logic (e.g., the law of identity), but also praxeological ones. Argumentation is not just free-floating propositions but always involves also at least two distinct arguers, a proponent and an opponent, i.e., argumentation is a subcategory of human action.*

Praxeology is the system of logical implications based on the axiomatic fact of human action, i.e., a series of propositions whose validity does not depend on historical experience, but which can be established by the intellectual apprehension or comprehension of the nature of things.[120] Hoppe is saying here that performative contradictions arise not only with logical presuppositions, but also with those involving human action, i.e., praxeological ones. We'll see how next:

> *Third, it is then shown that the mutual recognition of the principle of original appropriation, by both proponent and opponent, constitutes the praxeological presupposition of argumentation. No one can propose anything and expect his opponent to convince himself of the validity of this proposition or else deny it and propose something else unless his and his opponent's right to exclusive control over their "own" originally appropriated body (brain, vocal chords, etc.) and its respective standing room were already presupposed and assumed as valid.*

The very act of framing or considering an argument (about anything at all) presupposes the principle of original appropriation, that is, the ownership of that with which one carries out this act – one's own body and mind. When you propose an argument to someone, you necessarily put him to the task of either agreeing or disagreeing with you; therefore, by your action you're implicitly admitting from the start that he owns his body and mind, and by considering your argument

---

120 For further reading, see Murray N. Rothbard, *Praxeology: The Methodology of Austrian Economics*, http://mises.org/rothbard/praxeology.pdf.

he makes the same admission. It is implicitly recognized by the act of argumentation *that* the act of argumentation is not possible unless one does own his body and mind.

> *Finally, if the recognition of the principle of original appropriation forms the praxeological presupposition of argumentation, then it is impossible to provide a propositional justification for any other ethical principle without running thereby into performative contradictions.*

The act of proposing any argument that one does not own one's own body and mind therefore proves the proposition wrong by its very performance. Therefore, it is praxeologically impossible to provide a propositional justification for any ethical system that denies the principle of original appropriation.

APPENDIX B

THE BIBLICAL BASIS FOR A LIBERTARIAN SOCIETY

If God is the author of liberty, he would know better than anyone what form of government is suitable for preserving the liberty he gave us. Therefore, if you want to find a model for a government that will preserve your liberty, it only makes sense to look at the government of ancient Israel.

In ancient Israel, before the rise of the kings, there was no distinction between the criminal law and the civil law, and there was only one branch of government – the judiciary. There was no executive,[121] no prosecutor, and no police. Law enforcement was an individual or community affair not delegated to unrelated persons. No one had any particular privilege or authority over anyone else to enforce the laws and regulations, and all laws applied to everyone equally.[122]

The laws were given directly by God, and disputes among citizens were settled by judges. When the need for new rules arose, they were established on a case-by-case

---

121 The executive branch of government is the one charged with enforcing the law; it is composed of a class of citizens that have the special privilege of using force against other citizens. In ancient Israel there were no such privileges.

122 The exception was the priestly class of Levites, which reflected the theocratic basis of the law of the Israelites. Thus, the nation of Israel was structurally libertarian in its stateless civil governance, and familial in its moral governance. We will leave for another day an in-depth explanation, but for now I'll observe that this is a logical extension of God's claim on the Israelites as "his people." Just as the head of the family establishes the moral code of his family, so did God establish a moral code for his nation.

basis – this was essentially the "legal precedent" system of justice that characterized the common law of England and the United States.

Legislation was forbidden. The judges and teachers of the law could interpret the law, extract principles from it, and apply them to new situations not specified in the law, but they could neither add to nor subtract from the law.

There was no standing army. When the time came to fight, citizens took up their own arms and went to battle. Military service was not compulsory, although there was no doubt a significant element of peer pressure that discouraged cowardice.

Criminals were prosecuted by the victim or his relatives, not by a prosecutor, and there was no such thing as a fine; any money paid by the criminal went to the victim as restitution. If he couldn't afford it, he worked it off as the victim's personal slave.

So originally there was no legislature, no executive, no prosecutor, and no police. In short, there was no state.

But that's not to say there was no governance. There was a body of law regulating civil and criminal matters; there were judges who settled disputes between citizens of the nation; there was a civil order; there were territories with defined boundaries, property rights and obligations, standardized weights and measures, and so on. But all of these elements of civilization were administered without a state.

Of course, it was too good to last. In the time of Samuel things took a bad turn as the people rejected God's way of liberty and demanded a king to rule over them, like other nations had. Samuel warned them that they would not like the results, but the people insisted, and God obliged them (hence the old adage, "be careful what you pray for"). Read 1 Samuel chapter 8 and you'll find that our own government is in some ways even worse than the wicked government of the kings that Samuel warned them about:

10 And Samuel told all the words of the LORD unto the people that asked of him a king.

11 And he said, This will be the manner of the king that shall reign over you: He will take your sons, and appoint [them] for himself, for his chariots, and [to be] his horsemen; and [some] shall run before his chariots.

12 And he will appoint him captains over thousands, and captains over fifties; and [will set them] to ear his ground, and to reap his harvest, and to make his instruments of war, and instruments of his chariots.

13 And he will take your daughters [to be] confectionaries, and [to be] cooks, and [to be] bakers.

14 And he will take your fields, and your vineyards, and your oliveyards, [even] the best [of them], and give [them] to his servants.

15 And he will take the tenth of your seed, and of your vineyards, and give to his officers, and to his servants.

16 And he will take your menservants, and your maidservants, and your goodliest young men, and your asses, and put [them] to his work.

17 He will take the tenth of your sheep: and ye shall be his servants.

18 And ye shall cry out in that day because of your king which ye shall have chosen you; and the LORD will not hear you in that day.

19 Nevertheless the people refused to obey the voice of Samuel; and they said, Nay; but we will have a king over us;

20 That we also may be like all the nations; and that our king may judge us, and go out before us, and fight our battles.

The state is a manmade invention; it is not the natural order of creation. The concept of having some persons with the privilege of ruling over others is an old one, but that's not to say it's a good idea. If the account in Samuel tells us anything, it is that it has been a bad idea from the beginning. Add to that the fact that we do an even worse job of it than the early kings of Israel did (just compare our tax rates to the ones Samuel decried), and it leaves you wondering how we've accomplished anything at all in the last few millennia.

The founders of the United States understood that God created us to live free from the rule of other men, and they established a government whose job was limited to the protection of liberty. But it seems that now the American people have been seduced by the old idea that they need kings to rule them, and the government has become the greatest *violator* of our liberties.

When people don't trust their creator to provide their needs, they look for provision elsewhere. In God's design, a liberty-based socioeconomic system will provide food, shelter, and clothing for all its members, but those who don't believe this look for a substitute to provide their needs. They have given up liberty under God and replaced it with dependence on the state.

When free men encounter a problem, they use their God-given liberty to find a solution. The solution might lie in the way God designed family and community, or in the way he designed liberty-based economies to generate wealth and eliminate poverty. Or if the problem is of man's own doing, the solution might lie in the fact that the men who caused their own problem now suffer the consequences of their actions; others see it and learn not to behave the same way.

FOOTNOTES

1 Paul Joseph Watson, "TSA Gives Rapists And Illegals The Green Light While Groping Children," *Alex Jones' Prison Planet*, Nov. 10, 2010 (http://www.prisonplanet.com/tsa-gives-rapists-and-illegals-the-green-light-while-groping-children.html).

2 Tonyaa Weathersbee, "Barber Shop Raids Recall Days of Slavery," *Black America Web*, Dec. 15, 2010 (http://www.blackamericaweb.com/?q=articles%2Fnews%2Fbaw_commentary_news%2F24305&sms_ss=facebook&at_x).

3 P.J. Huffstutter, "Raw Milk Raid Highlights A Hunger," *Los Angeles Times*, July 25, 2010 (http://articles.latimes.com/2010/jul/25/business/la-fi-raw-food-raid-20100725). Watch a video of the raid at *Republic Broadcasting Network* (http://republicbroadcasting.org/?p=9870). On the health benefits of raw milk, see Randolph Jonsson, "Finally! Raw Milk Information You Can Trust!" *Raw Milk Facts* (http://www.raw-milk-facts.com/index.html). On the negative health consequences of pasteurization laws, see Kerri Knox, "The Long Term Health Consequences of Pasteurized Milk Laws, *Easy Immune System Health Blog*, (http://blog.easy-immune-health.com/digestive-health/the-long-term-health-consequences-of-pasteurized-milk-laws). The Weston A. Price Foundation is one of the most important sources of information about natural foods and nutrition; http://www.westonaprice.org.

4 As of this writing, 2009 is the latest year for which Planned Parenthood has published figures. Penny Starr, "Planned Parenthood Reports Abortion Rate Up By More Than 8,000 in One Year," *CNS News*, March 7, 2011 (http://www.cnsnews.com/news/article/planned-parenthood-reports-record-aborti).

5 Laurence Kotlikoff, "U.S. Is Bankrupt and We Don't Even Know It: Laurence Kotlikoff," Bloomberg News, Aug. 10, 2010 (http://www.bloomberg.com/news/2010-08-11/u-s-is-bankrupt-and-we-don-t-even-know-commentary-by-laurence-kotlikoff.html). I don't know the math to verify this stunning claim, but because of his credentials I don't reject it out of hand. Laurence J. Kotlikoff is a William Fairfield Warren Professor at Boston University, a Professor of Economics at Boston University, a Fellow of the American Academy of Arts and Sciences, a Fellow of the Econometric Society, a Research Associate of the National Bureau of Economic Research, President of Economic Security Planning, Inc., a company specializing in financial planning software, a columnist for Bloomberg, a columnist for Forbes, and a blogger for The Economist. Professor Kotlikoff received his B.A. in Economics from the University of Pennsylvania in 1973 and his Ph.D. in Economics from Harvard University in 1977.

From 1977 through 1983 he served on the faculties of economics of the University of California, Los Angeles and Yale University. In 1981-82 Professor Kotlikoff was a Senior Economist with the President's Council of Economic Advisers.

Professor Kotlikoff is author or co-author of 14 books and hundreds of professional journal articles.

Professor Kotlikoff publishes extensively in newspapers and magazines on issues of financial reform, personal finance, taxes, Social Security, healthcare, deficits, generational accounting, pensions, saving, and insurance.

Professor Kotlikoff has served as a consultant to the International Monetary Fund, the World Bank, the Harvard Institute for International Development, the Organization for Economic Cooperation and Development, the Swedish Ministry of Finance, the Norwegian Ministry of Finance, the Bank of Italy, the Bank of Japan, the Bank of England, the Government of Russia, the Government of Ukraine, the Government of Bolivia, the Government of Bulgaria, the Treasury of New Zealand, the Office of Management and Budget, the U.S. Department of Education, the U.S. Department of Labor, the Joint Committee on Taxation, The Commonwealth of Massachusetts, The American Council of Life Insurance, Merrill Lynch, Fidelity Investments, AT&T, AON Corp., and other major U.S. corporations.

He has provided expert testimony on numerous occasions to committees of Congress including the Senate Finance Committee, the House Ways and Means Committee, and the Joint Economic Committee.

6 William Norman Grigg, "Stormtroopers and Child-Snatchers," *LewRockwell.com*, April 13, 2011 (http://www.lewrockwell.com/grigg/grigg-w206.html).

7 This doesn't even address the hidden costs of engine damage caused by government-mandated ethanol/gasoline formulations.

8 U.S. Constitution, Article 1, Section 8.

9 317 U.S. 111 (1942).

10 This is not hyperbole. Imagine that we're victims of a pandemic flu, and the government issues emergency regulations "in the public interest." Among these might be mandatory flu shots, face masks, and certain mandatory hygienic practices such as hand-washing and the use of facial tissues, perhaps only FDA approved tissues manufactured by a small cartel of Big Pharma companies. Not so hard to imagine, is it?

11 A statist is one who believes that the state, instead of the private sector, is the solution to economic, social, and cultural problems.

12 See Judicial Watch Press Release, "Judicial Watch Uncovers New Documents Detailing Pelosi's Use of Air Force Aircraft," Jan. 28, 2010

(http://www.judicialwatch.org/news/2010/jan/judicial-watch-uncovers-new-documents-detailing-pelosis-use-air-force-aircraft).

13 Marc Tapscott, "President and family on multi-million dollar Christmas vacation in Hawaii," *The Washington Examiner*, Dec. 29, 2010 (http://washingtonexaminer.com/blogs/beltway-confidential/2010/12/president-and-family-multi-million-dollar-christmas-vacation-hawa). Obama and the 111th Congress are not the first to abuse the taxpayer's money – that has been going on for a long time. They're just more brazen about it now, because the public is numb, and government spending has become a juggernaut.

14 Cartel: A small group of individuals or companies with control of a market.

15 The fact that the guns and engines of war are in the hands of the citizens is the only thing that has restrained the state in Switzerland for more than seven centuries, and liberty is threatened even there, as the state chips inexorably away at the right of citizens to be armed. In the United States, the rise of totalitarian government is directly tied to the virtual death – at the hands of the state – of the Second Amendment.

16 If it didn't have a monopoly it wouldn't be a government, but a private security force competing in a free market against other security producers, or else it would need to have a government to grant it a monopoly on violence, because the only way to sustain a monopoly on violence is by government-supplied violence. But this latter situation is a distinction without meaning; the monopolistic security force is subsumed in the government. Thus we see that government and monopolistic violence go hand in hand.

17 Imprimatur: Official sanction or approval.

18 Murray N. Rothbard, *The Ethics of Liberty*, (New York: New York University Press, 2002), 180.

19 Hans-Hermann Hoppe, *Democracy: The God That Failed* (New Brunswick: Transaction Publishers, 2001), 45.

20 Read about Project Gunrunner. John Solomon, David Heath and Gordon Witkin, "Whistleblower Says Agents Strongly Objected to Risky Strategy," *Center For Public Integrity iWatch News*, March 4, 2011 (http://www.publicintegrity.org/articles/entry/2976/).

21 Just consider how the definition of "terrorism" has expanded in Western democracies since 2001. Today it includes, among many others, mere criticism of public officials (http://dir.groups.yahoo.com/group/LibertyStudents/message/1739); counterfeiting, see Federal Bureau of Investigation, Defendant Convicted of Minting His Own Currency, http://www.fbi.gov/charlotte/press-releases/2011/defendant-convicted-of-minting-

his-own-currency (March 18, 2011); biker gang membership, see Nicholas Broadbent, "The Expanding Definition of 'Terrorist,'" *NewMatilda.com*, April 6, 2009 (http://newmatilda.com/2009/04/06/expanding-definition-terrorist); and violence against government officials, disruptive activities or threats thereof against computer networks, assassination or kidnapping with the intent to affect government policy (USA PATRIOT Act).

22 On the cost and social benefits of road and highway privatization see Walter Block, *The Privatization of Roads and Highways*, (Auburn: Ludwig von Mises Institute. 2009). There have been many private road systems in the United States and other countries, and even today there are some private toll roads in operation. However, they face a competitive disadvantage against government subsidized roads; a taxpayer is already heavily invested in the public road and is, therefore, reluctant to pay an additional toll for road use.

23 Taxation is just institutional theft. That is, when we tax people, we take money from them against their will, by force. This is theft, by definition, but when we do it through government action, we pretend that it's legitimate.24 Etymology: The origin and historical development of the meaning of words.

25 The US government pays to destroy crops grown by small farmers, and in every practical sense this policy *benefits* the drug traders. In Bolivia, Peru, Afghanistan, and other drug-farming countries, soldiers burst out of the woods and shoot farmers, burn houses, and destroy crops, all at the behest of the US. The drug traders welcome this practice; the demand for their product remains fixed, and the price of their stockpiles increases (especially with opiates, which have a shelf life of several years). The large traders move production to other areas and now control the production directly. The farmers who once realized capital gains now work the traders' farms as hired labor. The traders realize economies of scale and of vertical integration; their profits increase, but the small farmers suffer. See, e.g., Constance Garcia-Barrio, "U.S. War on Drugs in Colombia is Ravaging Farmers and Land," *Common Dreams*, March 26, 2001 (http://www.commondreams.org/views01/0326-03.htm); Barnett R. Rubin and Omar Zakhilwal, "A War On Drugs, Or A War On Farmers?" *Wall Street Journal*, Jan. 11, 2005 (www.cic.nyu.edu/peacebuilding/oldpdfs/Farmers.pdf); Graham Gori, "War on drugs leaves poor Bolivian farmers hungry, desperate," *Miami Herald*, Aug. 31, 2003 (http://www.latinamericanstudies.org/bolivia/bolivia-drugs-03.htm).

26 Wikipedia, *War On Drugs*, (http://en.wikipedia.org/wiki/War_on_Drugs).

27 Wikipedia, *Incarceration In The United States*, (http://en.wikipedia.org/wiki/Incarceration_in_the_United_States).

28 Office of National Drug Control Policy, *Drug Use Trends*, http://www. whitehousedrugpolicy.gov/publications/factsht/druguse/ (October 2002).

29 David DeGraw, "The 'War On Drugs' Is A $2.5 Trillion Racket: How Big Banks, Private Military Companies And The Prison Industry Cash In," *Real News Reporter,* July 10, 2011 (http://www.realnewsreporter. com/?p=6248).

30 The market for independent arbitration services provides partial relief from the government monopoly on civil judicial administration, but it suffers from serious flaws compared to a completely free market for judicial services. First, the government court is already subsidized by your taxes, so when you hire the arbitrator's services you're essentially paying twice for justice. Second, the arbitrator's rulings are not much better in quality than the government's, because even he is mostly bound to the laws produced by the government. Finally, as long as there are state-run courts, there will always be a demand for bad justice, because it can be used to obtain advantages unavailable in a good judicial system (e.g., one rich participant who can afford the proceedings vs. a poor one who can't), or just to torment a legal opponent out of vindictiveness. We wouldn't have this problem in a freely competitive market – in that system, both participants must consent to jurisdiction.

31 Jane Wells, "Steve Wynn Takes on Washington, Vegas & EBITDA," *CNBC News*, May 28, 2010 (http://www.cnbc.com/id/37392344/Steve_ Wynn_Takes_on_Washington_Vegas_EBITDA) Watch the video at http:// www.truthaboutliberty.com/economics/steve-wynn-on-the-economy/.

32 Bryan Mims, "Lunchbox mix-up leads to charges for Sanford student," *WRAL.com*, Dec. 28, 2010 (http://www.wral.com/news/local/ story/8845676/).

33 Government schools don't teach this kind of thing because if enough people were actually educated, they'd reject destructive government policies, thereby depriving politicians of the power they are addicted to. Private schools, including home schools, don't teach this stuff either, but only because the knowledge has been almost lost. Fortunately for our children, a few have retained this knowledge. Do your part and spread it as far and wide as possible.

34 Hans-Hermann Hoppe, *Democracy: The God that Failed*, (New Jersey: Transaction Publishers, 2001), p. 30, fn. 30.

35 Id. at 31, fn. 31.

36 Laurence Kotlikoff, "U.S. Is Bankrupt and We Don't Even Know It: Laurence Kotlikoff," *Bloomberg News*, Aug. 10, 2010 (http://www. bloomberg.com/news/2010-08-11/u-s-is-bankrupt-and-we-don-t-even-know-commentary-by-laurence-kotlikoff.html). For a list of Dr. Kotlikoff's impressive credentials, see footnote 5.

37 The Cartel, official web site (http://www.thecartelmovie.com/cgi-local/content.cgi?g=27).

38 By some estimates, Federal education spending in 2010 was nearly $160 billion. See, e.g., Christopher Chantrill, "US Federal Budget Analyst," *USGovernmentSpending.com*, (http://www.usgovernmentspending.com/education_budget_2011_2.html).

39 Steve Watson, "The Police State Takeover of Schools, *Alex Jones' Infowars.net*, July 24, 2007 (http://www.infowars.net/articles/july2007/240707Schools.htm).

40 Id.

41 Id.

42 Matthew Lysiak, Kate Nocera, and Larry McShane, "Laura Timoney fumes after son Patrick, 9, is busted for bringing 2-inch-long toy gun to PS 52,) *New York Daily News*, Feb. 4, 2010 (http://www.nydailynews.com/ny_local/education/2010/02/04/2010-02-04_big_trouble_over_this_tiny_toy_mom_fuming_at_a_lack_of_common_sense_as_son_buste.html).

43 Elissa Harrington, "School Makes Boy Take American Flag Off Bike,) *KTXL Fox 40 News*, Nov. 12, 2010 (http://www.fox40.com/news/headlines/ktxl-americanflagbike111122010,0,3045879.htmlstory).

44 A 2008 study by the National Center for Education Statistics reports that about 1.5 million children were being homeschooled in the United States. http://www.nces.ed.gov/pubs2009/2009030.pdf.

45 James T. Harris, "Obama Stash," http://www.youtube.com/watch?v=_Ojd13kZlCA&feature=related (Oct. 15, 2009).

46 Further reading: James Bailey Brislin, "Government Housing Programs Incubate Crime, Social Problem," *The Carpet City Chronicle*, Aug. 14, 2008 (http://carpetcity.wordpress.com/2008/08/14/goverment-housing-programs/); Tim Montgomerie, "A strong family and small state ought to go hand in hand," *The Telegraph*, March 17, 2009 (http://www.telegraph.co.uk/comment/5008047/A-strong-family-and-small-state-ought-to-go-hand-in-hand.html).

47 See, e.g., Don Mathews, "The Free Market: Lifting All Boats," *The Freeman*, April 1997 (http://www.thefreemanonline.org/featured/the-free-market-lifting-all-boats/).

48 Conn Carroll, "True Cost of Stimulus: $3.27 Trillion," The Foundry, Feb. 12, 2009 (http://blog.heritage.org/2009/02/12/true-cost-of-stimulus-327-trillion/).

49 A Lame Duck session of Congress happens in even numbered years after the elections. Outgoing representatives (those who lost the election)

are leaving anyway, so they don't care what the voters think about how they vote on legislation. Lame Duck sessions are particularly bad when the party in control loses the election; they're still in control of the congress and sometimes pass horrendous legislation in a fit of rage against the voters who ousted them. Lame Duck sessions became possible in 1933 with the passage of the 17th Amendment; as originally written, the Constitution did not allow for them.

50 A subsidy is a wealth transfer by the government to an industry or other economic sector that does not support itself. Welfare payments to individuals are subsidies of whatever economic factors resulted in the "poverty" the welfare payment is meant to alleviate. For example, unemployment compensation subsidizes unemployment. You always get more of whatever you subsidize, so this results in more unemployment.51 See Chapter 2: *The Kings of America*.

52 There are many forces arrayed against the health of the family unit. One of the most powerful is tax policy. The income tax and the death tax combine to make it extremely difficult for you to accumulate wealth that would benefit your succeeding generations. In fact, our entire monetary system, with its deliberate inflationary policy, is designed to confiscate your wealth over time. Other anti-family forces include state-controlled education, state supremacy in medical matters, and state control of housing and food.

53 See, e.g., "New research: How Traditional Families Help Children Succeed," *Liturgical*, July 24, 2009 (http://liturgical.wordpress. com/2009/07/24/new-research-how-traditional-families-help-children-conservative-values-education/).

54 *Sine qua non* is Latin for "without which nothing." It identifies something that is indispensable for the existence of something else.

55 Scott Walker, "Why I'm Fighting In Wisconsin," *The Wall Street Journal*, Mar. 10, 2011 (http://online.wsj.com/article/SB1000142405274870 4132204576190260787805984.html).

56 The US was established as a republic, but it has always had a democratic electoral process. As suffrage has been expanded over the last two centuries, the republican structure has been weakened and the democratic characteristics have worsened.

57 On the characteristics of monarchies and democracies, read the excellent book by Hoppe, *Democracy: The God that Failed*.

58 Again, I'm talking about the character of the system – some individual elected officials do in fact care about the value of the currency, but they eventually lose to opponents who get elected by promising to give away more stuff. It's harder to raise taxes than it is to devalue (inflate) the

currency, so politicians always inflate as much as they can. This makes more money available for them to spend right now, even though it will be worth a little less tomorrow.

59 Suffrage: the right to vote.

60 The anti-federalists vigorously argued against the enumerated powers themselves, considering them alone to be too broad, (see, e.g., Anti-Federalist Paper No. 17), but I'm not aware of any of them arguing that the federal government would frankly ignore its Constitutional limitations.

61 Hoppe, *Democracy: The God that Failed*, 42.

62 "Fake gold and silver Ron Paul coins seized," MSNBC.com, Nov. 16, 2007 (http://www.msnbc.msn.com/id/21836699/ns/politics-decision_08/); Federal Bureau of Investigation, *Defendant Convicted of Minting His Own Currency,* http://charlotte.fbi.gov/dojpressrel/pressrel11/ce031811.htm (March 11, 2011).

63 Media Malpractice, official web site (http://www.howobamagotelected.com/).

64 Wall Street Journal Digital Network, "Rahm Emanuel on the Opportunities of Crisis," http://www.youtube.com/watch?v=_mzcbXi1Tkk.

65 See, e.g., NRA Videos, "NRA: The Untold Story of Gun Confiscation After Katrina," http://www.youtube.com/watch?v=-taU9d26wT4&feature=related (March 7, 2007).

66 Lone Lantern, "Staff Sergeant Refuses Gun Grab - Reality Report Special Interview," http://www.youtube.com/watch?v=uLaKsbM0x3g (May 19, 2010).

67 Jordy Yager, "Next step for tight security could be trains, boats, metro," *The Hill*, Nov. 23, 2010 (http://thehill.com/homenews/administration/130549-next-step-for-body-scanners-could-be-trains-boats-and-the-metro-).

68 Fredreka Schouten, "Body scanner makers doubled lobbying cash over 5 years," *USA Today*, Nov. 23, 2010 (http://www.usatoday.com/news/washington/2010-11-22-scanner-lobby_N.htm). The CEO of the company that manufactures one of these machines was one of President Obama's guests on his recent trip to India. OSI Systems Press Release, "Body Scanner Manufacturer Accompanies Obama on Trip to India," *Public Intelligence*, Nov. 10, 2010 (http://publicintelligence.net/body-scanner-manufacturer-accompanies-obama-on-trip-to-india/). This taxpayer-funded trip reportedly cost $200 million per day, and included a coterie of 3000 people. Press Trust of India, "US to spend $200 mn a day on Obama's Mumbai visit," *NDTV*, Nov. 2, 2010 (http://www.ndtv.com/article/india/us-to-spend-200-mn-a-day-on-obama-s-mumbai-visit-64106). A White

House spokesman denied that report, but refused to specify the cost. Chris McGreal, "Claim that Barack Obama's India visit will cost $200m a day is 'wildly inflated,'" *The Guardian*, Nov. 4, 2010 (http://www.guardian.co.uk/world/2010/nov/04/barack-obama-india-visit-cost-claim).

69 "Snow Comparison," *Snopes*, Jan. 11, 2011 (http://www.snopes.com/katrina/soapbox/snowfall.asp).

70 WSJDigitalNetwork, (Rahm Emanuel on the Opportunities of Crisis," http://www.youtube.com/watch?v=_mzcbXi1Tkk (Nov. 19, 2008).

71 "A 40-Year Wish List," *The Wall Street Journal*, Jan. 28, 2009 (http://online.wsj.com/article/SB123310466514522309.html).

72 Conn Carroll, "True Cost of Stimulus: $3.27 Trillion," The Foundry, Feb. 12, 2009 (http://blog.heritage.org/2009/02/12/true-cost-of-stimulus-327-trillion/).

73 ThinkFY, "Obama: Shovel-Ready Not as Shovel-Ready as We Expected," http://youtu.be/O55aRrvXtio (June 13, 2011).

74 Andrew Pollack, Anxiety Over Radiation Drives a Sales Surge for a Drug Against Thyroid Cancer," *The New York Times*, March 15, 2011 (http://www.nytimes.com/2011/03/16/health/16iodide.html).

75 Yes, some individual public teachers work hard to provide a good education because of their good moral character, and in that sense they reap an altruistic profit, but I'm talking about the irresistible forces of economics and their ultimate effect on the quality and nature of government services. To those teachers who are not cynically careless of their teaching duties, I would just point out that public education by its very nature is harmful to children, families, and civilization in general, because it discourages parental involvement in their child's upbringing, thereby bringing on a decline in the quality of families in society. So, however well they may do their teaching job, their very participation in the public education system is harmful to us all.

76 Hoppe, *Democracy: The God that Failed*, 100.

77 The fact that a state government might pay the salary and the federal government collect the tax is irrelevant, because that is merely a bookkeeping entry in the transaction between one level of government and another, both of whom contribute to the salaries of public employees in the form of grants and direct subsidies.

78 Sara Murray, "In U.S., 14% Rely on Food Stamps," *The Wall Street Journal*, Nov. 4, 2010 (http://blogs.wsj.com/economics/2010/11/04/some-14-of-us-uses-food-stamps/).

79 John Mellowy, "Welfare State: Handouts Make Up One-Third of U.S. Wages," *CNBC*, Mar. 8, 2011 (http://www.cnbc.com/id/41969508/).

80 Elizabeth MacDonald, "Government Cash Handouts Now Top Tax Revenues," *Fox News*, April 10, 2011 (http://www.foxbusiness.com/markets/2011/04/20/government-cash-handouts-exceed-tax-revenues/).

81 I wish to thank Richard Maybury for his excellent book on this subject, *World War II: The Rest Of The Story*, (Placerville: Bluestocking Press, 2003).

82 R.J. Rummel, *Death by Government* (New Brunswick: Transaction Publishers, 1994).

83 Id.

84 Id.

85 Martin van Creveld, *Supplying War*, (Cambridge: Cambridge University Press, 1977).

86 This is why military historians have the pithy saying, "amateurs focus on strategy; experts focus on logistics."

87 This is despite the fact that violent crime has decreased since the mid-1990s, possibly due to a resurgence at the State level of the right to carry concealed weapons. The government has simply shifted its focus to non-violent crimes.

88 A complete study of the political parties and their influence is beyond the scope of this chapter. Thanks to Richard J. Maybury for his clarity of thinking on this issue; many of the ideas in this chapter are developed from his excellent book, *Are You Liberal? Conservative? or Confused?* (Placerville: Bluestocking Press, 2004).

89 Larry O'Connor, "Which Part of the Constitution is 'Confusing' Ezra?" *Big Journalism*, Dec. 30, 2010 (http://bigjournalism.com/sright/2010/12/30/which-part-of-the-constitution-is-confusing-ezra/).

90 Tim Fernhoz, "CBO Says Budget Deal Will Cut Spending by Only $352 Million This Year," *National Journal*, April 14, 2011 (http://www.nationaljournal.com/budget/cbo-says-budget-deal-will-cut-spending-by-only-352-million-this-year-20110413).

91 Alister Bull and Jeff Mason, "Obama's 2010 budget: deficit soars amid job spending," *Reuters*, Feb. 1, 2010 (http://www.reuters.com/article/2010/02/01/idUSN31157907). Actually, the rate was over $1.6 trillion per year during the first two years of Obama administration leading up to this budget deal. Terence P. Jeffrey, "Federal Borrowing on Pace to Hit Debt Limit in Less Than Week," *CNSNews.com*, April 20, 2011 (http://www.cnsnews.com/news/article/federal-borrowing-pace-hit-debt-limit-le).

92 Erik Wasson and Pete Kasperowicz, "House passes Ryan's '12 budget; conservatives want more cuts," *The Hill*, April 15, 2011 (http://thehill.com/

blogs/on-the-money/budget/156379-house-clears-ryans-2012-budget-plan-conservatives-want-more-cuts).

93 Hoppe, *Democracy: The God That Failed*, 187-188.

94 Id. at 203.

95 See ch. 17, *The American Form of Government*.

96 Indeed, most of the leading libertarian thinkers were social-cultural conservatives. See Hoppe, *Democracy: The God That Failed*, 202.

97 Id.

98 For a more detailed discussion of the Biblical basis for a libertarian philosophy, see Appendix B.

99 See Appendix A for a discussion of the proof of this universal law of ethics.

100 Again, this only addresses your rights, not your moral obligations. Even in an ideal libertarian society, your refusal to save a drowning man would have undesirable consequences. You'd be reviled and discriminated against, or shunned. The government wouldn't be permitted to punish you, but your friends, family, and acquaintances might well refuse to have any further dealings with you.

101 Murray N. Rothbard, *The Ethics of Liberty* (New York: New York University Press, 2002), 98.

102 There is a special case for abandonment. If Crusoe abandons the shelter, it becomes unowned. If someone else finds it, he may put it to use and thus acquires complete title by a new appropriation. Later we'll discuss the consequences of a father's abandoning his property rights, if any, to the fetus.

103 Rothbard, *The Ethics of Liberty*, 100.

104 A collateral benefit of eliminating all state involvement in the care and upbringing of the child is that it places a greater value on family and community relationships. To the extent that parents can rely on the state to take over in cases of difficulty with the children, they have less need for the help of family and friends. If, on the other hand, they can't fall back on the state, then family, friends, neighbors, and charities become more valuable. Relationships in general become more valuable, and in order to "purchase" more and better relationships, the parents make themselves more attractive to others. This encourages civility, nobility, generosity, hospitality – in fact, all the indicators of good neighborliness.

105 Id. at 98.

106 "Fee simple" means complete title, total ownership of all possible property rights.

107 It is not necessary for this discussion to delineate those rights. For Rothbard's discussion on this point, see Rothbard, *The Ethics of Liberty*, especially ch. 14: Children and Rights, pp. 97-112.

108 Rothbard argues that under libertarian law, "capital punishment would have to be confined strictly to the crime of murder." Id. at 85. Without agreeing or disagreeing with this point, it is sufficient to point out that the unborn child is not capable of murder or any other crime.

109 A blanket party is a means of corporal punishment conducted by a peer group, such as the military. The victim is covered with a blanket and struck repeatedly.

110 This obnoxious person might be a member of a very activist and fanatical pro-life group, but I mention this only to make the point that a truly free society would, in this way, minimize the impact of the societal fringe groups. Environmentalist nuts, animal rights thugs, militant pro-choicers, homeless bums, and homosexual rights activists would not be rewarded for their anti-social positions, as they are in a democratic society like ours, which provides a political "gravy train" for every variety of social deviancy. The democratic process stimulates social dysfunction and deviancy and is in this way decivilizing, whereas a free society naturally stimulates socially functional norms, and is in this way civilizing. Indeed, to get your way in a democratic society, you have to march, vandalize, make noise, and get in people's faces. The more obnoxious and repulsive you are, the more money and privilege you get from the state; you don't win people to your cause, you just find a politician who will trade some of his power, privilege, and money in exchange for your vote. To get your way in a free society, you have to be noble, persuasive, and in every way attractive, in order to win people to your cause voluntarily.

111 See ch. 6: *Can We Limit Government?*

112 Of course, the systemically dysfunctional apparatus of the Republican Party will itself be a mighty impediment, if the Tea Party is successful in taking it over. They are entrenched in the Washington power structure, and tea party newbies are going to be told "you don't know how things are done around here." Their response needs to be, "we're not doing things that way anymore."

113 The Tea Party's public thrust is primarily fiscal, but this is a tactic to avoid an internal rift on the issue of abortion. The strategy is "fiscal responsibility, free markets, and limited government," and the tactic is to avoid the social issues. But the reality is that a very large bloc of tea partiers, likely a majority, are pro-life, and the next-largest group is pro-choice due to a mistaken belief that a consistent liberty-oriented ethic requires it. Many of them will actually be relieved to learn of their mistake.

114 Again, I say "simple," not "easy." The concept is not hard to grasp, although the execution might well involve a lot of effort.

115 Icorvi Ministries, official web site, http://www.icorvi.org/index.php; Pedersen Law & Dispute Resolution Corporation, official web site, http://www.pedersenlaw.com/christian_dispute_resolution.html; and the Institute for Christian Conciliation, official web site, http://www.peacemaker.net/site/c.nuIWL7MOJtE/b.5394441/k.BD56/Home.htm, are three of the many resources available.

116 Hamilton County Medical Examiner's Office, *Frequently Asked Questions of the Hamilton County Medical Examiner Office*, http://www.hamiltontn.gov/medicalexaminer/me%20office%20faqs.htm (accessed Aug. 16, 2011).

117 Rothbard, *The Ethics of Liberty*, 45.

118 The only way out of this quandary would be for all people to register advance consent for all possible contingencies, which would lead to chaos, or to limit advance permission to those circumstances necessary to protect the individual right of 100% self-ownership, which brings us full-circle to the postulated case.

119 Hoppe, *Democracy: The God That Failed*, 201, footnote.

120 For further reading, see Murray N. Rothbard, *Praxeology: The Methodology of Austrian Economics*, http://mises.org/rothbard/praxeology.pdf.

121 The executive branch of government is the one charged with enforcing the law; it is composed of a class of citizens that have the special privilege of using force against other citizens. In ancient Israel there were no such privileges.

122 The exception was the priestly class of Levites, which reflected the theocratic basis of the law of the Israelites. Thus, the nation of Israel was structurally libertarian in its stateless civil governance, and familial in its moral governance. We will leave for another day an in-depth explanation, but for now I'll observe that this is a logical extension of God's claim on the Israelites as "his people." Just as the head of the family establishes the moral code of his family, so did God establish a moral code for his nation.

CPSIA information can be obtained at www.ICGtesting.com
Printed in the USA
LVOW030031191011

251010LV00002BA/2/P